FEELINGS & EMOTIONS

Pulse

track: life issues

Amy Simpson

general editor
Kara Eckmann Powell

Gospel Light

God's word for a jr. high world

PUBLISHING STAFF
William T. Greig, Publisher
Dr. Elmer L. Towns, Senior Consulting Publisher
Pam Weston, Editor
Patti Pennington Virtue, Assistant Editor
Christi Goeser, Editorial Assistant
Kyle Duncan, Associate Publisher
Bayard Taylor, M.Div., Senior Editor, Biblical and Theological Issues
Dr. Gary S. Greig, Senior Advisor, Biblical and Theological Issues
Kevin Parks, Cover Designer
Rosanne Richardson, Cover Production
Debi Thayer, Designer
Jeff Mattesich and Siv Ricketts, Contributing Writers

ISBN 0-8307-2548-2
© 2000 by Gospel Light
All rights reserved.
Printed in the U.S.A.

Scripture quotations are taken from the *Holy Bible, New International Version*®. Copyright © 1973, 1978, 1984 by International Bible Society. Used by permission of Zondervan Publishing House. All rights reserved.

How To Make Clean Copies From This Book

PRAISE FOR PULSE

As a professor and trainer of youth ministers, this is the best concept for junior high discipleship that I have ever seen. I love this curriculum not only because it gets Scripture into the hands and hearts of junior highers, but it does it in a way that they can grab hold of and enjoy. There is none better than Kara Eckmann Powell to ensure the integrity, depth and appropriateness of this tool. The **Pulse** curriculum is going to be a landmark resource for years to come. —**Chapman R. Clark, Ph.D.**, Associate Professor of Youth and Family Ministry, Fuller Theological Seminary

What I really appreciate about the **Pulse** series is that it fleshes out what I consider to be two absolute essentials for great curriculum: biblical depth and active learning. It is obvious that this is a curriculum designed by youth workers who care about junior high kids and who deeply care about helping them grow in their walk with Jesus. —**Duffy Robbins**, Associate Professor, Department of Youth Ministry, Eastern College

The youth leader's biggest challenge today is to relevantly translate the gospel to this generation. Kara has written a game plan for doing just that! **Pulse** is a curriculum that will help God's Word to become real for your students and will help you to reach a diverse generation—from the edgy/techno savvy to the more conservative student. It will produce a life change in (you)th! —**Larry Acosta**, President, The Hispanic Ministry Center

Pulse will help youth leaders create a great learning environment, provide a solid biblical education and challenge students to practice their faith daily. If leaders will use the variety of learning activities and creative teaching ideas, they will bring excellence to every lesson while enjoying the benefit of a simplified preparation time. —**Lynn Ziegenfuss**, Vice President of People Development, Youth for Christ/USA

In a world where Truth has been hidden in tolerance and where God has become the god of one's choice, Truth and solid biblical principles must be imparted to our students. **Pulse** CAPITALIZES both God and Truth. It's real, it's relevant, and it's *the* Truth! —**Monty L. Hipp**, Youth Communicator, Creative Communications

This is the best junior high/middle school curriculum to come out in years. Students will love this curriculum. —**Jim Burns, Ph.D.**, President, YouthBuilders

Wow! I'm impressed with the quality and the message this curriculum brings to millennials. It's going to be fun to be with kids with this material! —**Charles Kim**, *JDM—Journey Devotional Magazine*, The Oriental Mission Church

Kara knows students, teaching, youth workers and the Bible; and she mixes that with a passion for God's Word. It seems that everything Kara touches is gold and I believe this **Pulse** curriculum not only bears her name but her touch as well. Thanks, Kara, for another great contribution to youth ministry! —**Doug Fields**, Youth Pastor of Saddleback Church and author of *Purpose Driven Youth Ministry*

Pulse
Feelings and Emotions

CONTENTSCONTENTSCONTENTSCONTENTSCONTENTS

Unit I: Things That Make Us Feel Good

Unit II: Things That Challenge Us

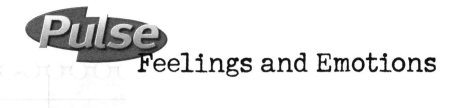

Dedication

To Cameron, who will be a teenager someday, thanks for waiting to be born until after I finished this project!

...You've Made the Right Choice in Choosing Pulse for Your Junior Highers

The Top Ten Reasons...

9. Junior highers need and deserve youth workers who are expert trainers and teachers of biblical truth.

Every book is pulsating with youth leader tips and a full-length youth worker article designed to infuse YOU with more passion and skill for your ministry to junior highers.

10. Junior highers equate who God is with what church is like. To them a boring youth ministry means a boring God.

Fun and variety are the twin threads that weave their way through this curriculum's every page.

8. Junior highers need ongoing reminders of the big idea of each session.

Wouldn't it be great if you could give your students devotionals every week to reinforce the learning goals of the session? Get this: YOU CAN because THIS CURRICULUM DOES.

7. Some of our world's most effective evangelists are junior highers.

Every session, and we mean EVERY session, concludes with an evangelism option that ties "the big idea" of the session to the big need to share Christ with others.

6. Since no two junior highers (or their leaders) look, think or act alike, no two junior high ministries look, think or act alike.

Each step comes with three options that you can cut and paste to create a session that works best for YOUR students and YOUR personality.

5. Junior highers' growing minds are ready for more than just fun and games with a little Scripture thrown in.

Scripture is the very skeleton of each session, giving it its shape, its form and its very life.

4. Junior highers learn best when they can see, taste, feel and experience the session.

This curriculum involves students in every step through active learning and games to prove to students that following Christ is the greatest adventure ever.

3. Tragically, most junior highers are under challenged in their walks with Christ.

We've packed the final step of each session with three options that serve to move students a few steps forward in their walks with Christ.

2. Junior highers tend to understand the Bible in bits and pieces and miss the big picture of all that God has done for them.

This curriculum follows a strategic three-year plan that walks junior highers through the Bible, stopping at the most important points along the way.

1. Junior highers are moving through all sorts of changes—from getting a new body to getting a new locker.

We've designed a curriculum that revolves around one simple vision: moving God's Word into a junior high world.

Moving Through Pulse

Since **Pulse** is vibrating with so many different learning activities, this guide will help you pick and choose the best possible options for *your* students.

THE SESSIONS

The six sessions are split into two stand-alone units, so you can choose to teach either three or six sessions at a time. Each session is geared to be 45 to 90 minutes long and is comprised of the following four steps.

IT'S YOUR MOVE

A training article for you, the youth worker, to show you *why* and *how* to see students' worlds changed by Christ to change the world.

STEP 1 — MOVING IN

This first step helps students focus in on the theme of the lesson in a fun and engaging way through three options:

 MOVE IT—An active learning experience that may or may not involve all of your students.

 CHAT ROOM—Provocative, clear and simple questions to get your students thinking and chatting.

 FUN AND GAMES—Zany, creative and competitive games that may or may not involve all of your students.

STEP 2 — MOVING UP

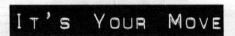

The second step enables students to look up to God by relating the very words of Scripture to the session topic through three options:

 MOVE IT—An active learning experience that may or may not involve all of your students.

 CHAT ROOM—Provocative, clear and simple questions to get your students chatting about the Scripture lesson.

 PULSE POINTS—A message outline with simple points and meaningful illustrations to give students some massive truths about Scripture with hardly any preparation on your part.

STEP 3
MOVING ON

This step asks students to look inward and discover how God's Word connects with their own worlds through three options:

 CHAT ROOM—Provocative, clear and simple questions to get your students chatting.

 REAL LIFE—A case study about someone (usually a junior higher) who needs your students' help figuring out what to do.

 TOUGH QUESTIONS—Four to six mind-stretching questions that challenge students to a new level of depth and integration.

STEP 4
MOVING OUT

This final step leads students out into their world with specific challenges to apply at school, at home and with their friends through three options based on your students' growth potential:

 LIGHT THE FIRE—For junior highers who may or may not be Christians and need easily accessible application ideas.

 FIRED UP—For students who are definitely Christians and are ready for more intense application ideas.

 SPREAD THE FIRE—A special evangelism application idea for students with a passion to see others come to know Christ.

OTHER IMPORTANT MOVING PARTS

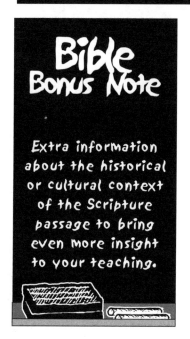

Bible Bonus Note

Extra information about the historical or cultural context of the Scripture passage to bring even more insight to your teaching.

Youth Leader Tip

Suggestions, options and/or other useful information to make your life easier or at least more interesting!

Devotions in Motion

WEEK FIVE: GRACE

Four devotionals for each session to keep the big idea moving through your junior highers' lives all week long.

ON THE MOVE—An appealing, easy-to-read handout you can give your junior highers to make sure they learn to appreciate their feelings and emotions as gifts from God, and use them in ways that glorify His Name.

Conquering Rocks & Boulders

It's Your Move

Think for a moment about some of your students. Literally picture them in your mind. Think of the most troublesome student you have, the one you've assigned his or her own personal adult staff member. Or think of your most attentive student, the one who sits near the front, gives you dead-on eye contact the whole time and volunteers to clean up the bus after retreats. Or maybe someone in between.

Now picture each of those students on a path—a desert path that is dry, dusty and lonely. Every day, your students wake up and step onto that path for a new emotional adventure.

Some days the path is smooth and easy. Those are the days when your students feel like they have friends they like and, more important, who like them. They wake up, look in the mirror and actually smile at what they see. They feel good about themselves; they feel good about those around them. They just plain feel good.

But those days are few and far between. Usually the path that students walk has a few rocks ahead. Maybe your students look into a mirror and dislike what they see. Or maybe they find out their friends had a sleepover and didn't invite them. Or maybe they're stressed out about their science homework and are sure that the teacher, who they describe as evil, has something against them.

But then there are those days when junior highers trudge down the path and are confronted not with mere rocks but huge emotional boulders that block their progress. Their friends are getting involved in sexual relationships, inviting them to do likewise. Or their parents are pressuring them to do more, be involved with more and get better grades. Or they're so lonely that they just don't feel like living anymore.

Here's one of our problems in junior high ministry: Our goal has degenerated into simply helping students dodge the rocks and boulders. As long as they can get out of the way quickly enough, we think we're victorious. And sadly, so do they.

What's wrong with that? you ask. At least they're surviving. You're right—survival is better than extermination. But does it match God's goal for our students? I think not.

I know some 12-, 13- and 14-year-old heroes that are doing more than dodging the emotional rocks and boulders hurtling toward them. They're taking steps forward, and they're bringing others along with them.

There's Kelly, an eighth grader with braces and a lisp who has mustered up enough courage to start a new Christian club on her campus.

And there's Jennifer, whose compassion motivates her to ask every week for prayer for a Buddhist friend who seems open to spiritual things but is drifting in the wrong direction.

We must not be satisfied with seeing junior highers dodge the emotional obstacles in front of them. We need to help them move forward and be changed by Christ to change the world. This curriculum is devoted to helping students experience triumph in the midst of their emotional highs and lows. Allow me to give you a few tips to help you maximize the effectiveness of the following six lessons.

Cover lessons in both units. For junior highers, emotions are a roller coaster. You've probably seen this with your students: They're bummed because they have to stop playing fuzz ball, but then you tell them that they're having ice cream at the end of the meeting, and they become ecstatic. As you are prayerfully choosing which of these six lessons you'll use, make sure you choose lessons that help students in times when they're wallowing in the valleys as well as skipping along the mountaintops.

Point out the humanness of the biblical characters you're studying. Unfortunately, biblical characters are often presented as so perfectly victorious that students are left scratching their heads, wondering how they could possibly relate to them. This book tries to avoid that distortion by clearly focusing on the despair of Judas, the agony of Job and the doubt of Jonah.

Divide and conquer. If you're not regularly meeting in small groups with your students, perhaps you should experiment with discussion-group clusters during this series. The smaller the group, the more that trust can build; the more trust that is built, the more honest the sharing; the deeper the sharing, the deeper the healing.

Leave plenty of time for response and application. The last two steps of each lesson help students answer the major question they're wrestling with regarding their feelings: *What do I do with what I feel right now?* Please, for the sake of the students, leave enough time at the end of the lesson for them to pin down an answer.

—Kara Eckmann Powell

Contributors

Jeff Mattesich, author of the student devotionals, has been working with junior high students for over six years. He has also worked at Forest Home Christian Conference Center in California and currently works at Lake Avenue Church in Pasadena, California. Jeff also attends Azusa Pacific University.

Siv Ricketts, author of the student article, "How to Leave a Mark on Your School," is a student ministries director, freelance writer and editor, living in San Diego, California. Siv and her husband, Dave, have been ministering to students together for the past six years and have recently been blessed with a new son, Corban.

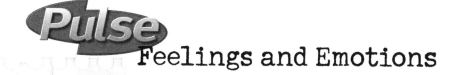 **Feelings and Emotions**

The Big Idea

There's only one true way to be content—to be in a growing relationship with Jesus.

Session Aims

In this session you will guide students to:

- Learn Paul's secret of being content no matter what the circumstances;
- Feel the need for contentment in their own lives;
- Respond by committing to finding contentment in Jesus this week.

The Biggest Verse

"I know what it is to be in need, and I know what it is to have plenty. I have learned the secret of being content in any and every situation, whether well fed or hungry, whether living in plenty or in want." Philippians 4:12

Other Important Verses

Acts 9:1-19; 27:39—28:6, 14-31;
2 Corinthians 11:24-29;
Philippians 1:13,14; 4:10-13

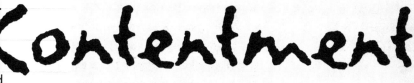
Contentment

STEP 1
MOVING IN

This step reminds students that everyone is looking for contentment.

Option 1 Move It

You'll need Magazines and newspapers, felt-tip pens, paper, scissors, glue, construction paper and other art supplies.

Ahead of time, set out the magazines and supplies.

When students arrive, greet them and ask them to create posters of their ideal lives. They can use any of the art supplies provided and be as creative as they want. Each person should create a poster that answers the question: **What would your life look like if it were perfect?**

When students are finished creating their posters, have them present their creations to everyone; then discuss:

What types of things would need to change in your life for you to find that perfect life pictured in your poster?

What is keeping you from experiencing that kind of life right now?

How does it feel to know what you want but be unable to get that life?

How does this perfect life on your poster make you feel about your life now?

Explain: **Everyone is looking for contentment. Usually, we look to our circumstances to make us feel content about our lives. As we start a new series about our feelings, we'll see that finding** *true* **contentment depends on looking for it in the right place.**

Option 2 Chat Room

You'll need A TV, a VCR and a blank videotape.

Ahead of time, record a segment or several clips from a TV shopping network program. **Option:** Collect an assortment of mail-order catalogs with a variety of merchandise.

Greet students and play the video clip (or pass around mail-order catalogs). Encourage students to pay attention to the kinds of products they see and the sales pitches.

Afterward, discuss:

What did they do to make the products we saw look appealing?

Why do you think we have entire TV networks devoted to buying and selling stuff? People are trying to buy happiness—materialism.

Why do you think retailers are so successful in our society? Good economy, materialism, etc.

Besides products, what are some other things we're always trying to get in life? **Why?** Friends, boyfriends, girlfriends, happiness, entertainment, etc.

Have you ever felt perfectly content with your life? For how long? What changed that feeling?

Explain: **One of the reasons people in our society are always buying things is because everyone is looking for contentment. Most of us believe we'll be happier and more content if we have more stuff or the right stuff. But that isn't where contentment comes from. As we'll see as we start a new series on feelings, finding true contentment depends on looking in the right place.**

Option 3 — Fun and Games

You'll need Five clothespins per student. **Optional:** A length of clothesline cord for the grand prize!

Greet students and give each one five clothespins. Have students pin the clothespins on their clothes where other people can see them and grab them. Explain that you're going to play a game for five minutes. The object of the game is to end up with as many clothespins as you can. To do this, players will grab clothespins from other people and put them on their own clothes. At the same time, however, other people will be trying to get their clothespins.

Play the game for five minutes and announce the winner (the player who ended the game with the most clothespins). Award the grand prize; then discuss:

How was this game like the way people tend to live in our society? They want what other people have; it shows selfishness and greed; etc.

Why do you think so many people are out to get as much as they can in life? They think they deserve it or that it will make them happy.

What are some of the things you think would make your life happier?

Have you ever felt perfectly content with your life? If so, how long did that feeling last?

If we can't find lasting contentment by getting more stuff, why do you think we keep trying? Because our culture tells us so.

Explain: **One of the reasons we're always trying to get more stuff is because everyone is looking for contentment. Even if our contentment doesn't last, we keep trying to find ways to make ourselves happy. But true contentment doesn't come from having a lot of stuff or living an easy life. As we'll see as we start a new series on feelings, finding true contentment depends on looking in the right place.**

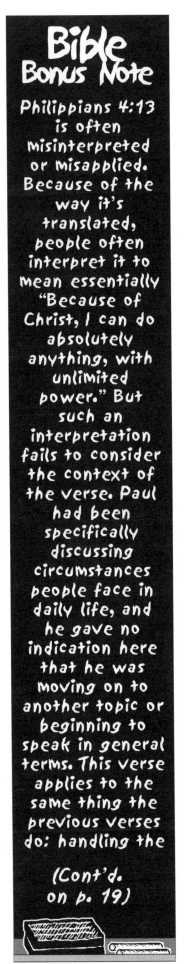

Bible Bonus Note

Philippians 4:13 is often misinterpreted or misapplied. Because of the way it's translated, people often interpret it to mean essentially "Because of Christ, I can do absolutely anything, with unlimited power." But such an interpretation fails to consider the context of the verse. Paul had been specifically discussing circumstances people face in daily life, and he gave no indication here that he was moving on to another topic or beginning to speak in general terms. This verse applies to the same thing the previous verses do: handling the

(Cont'd. on p. 19)

STEP 2 — MOVING UP

This step shows students how they can be content in spite of their circumstances.

Option 1  Move It

You'll need Several Bibles.

Divide students into four groups. Explain: **Today we're going to be studying part of the book of Philippians, a letter written by Paul to people who lived in a city called Philippi. But get this: Paul was in prison when he wrote it** (see Philippians 1:13,14), probably under house arrest in Rome (see Acts 28:14-31). **For two years, people could come and visit him, but he couldn't leave his house—ever. As you read Philippians 4:10-13, think about how you would feel if you were confined to your house.**

After they're finished reading, assign each group one verse from Philippians 4:10-13. Then ask each group to create a pantomime to illustrate the verse they've been assigned. No words can be used—just body movement and their best acting skills.

After groups have come up with their pantomimes, read Philippians 4:10-13. Have groups stand up and perform their pantomimes as you read the appropriate verses. Give a round of applause for the pantomimes; then discuss:

What different circumstances did Paul describe in this passage? Being in plenty or in need, well fed or hungry.

How did these circumstances affect Paul's life? What did Paul say he had learned? He learned to be content in any circumstance—good or bad.

What was Paul's secret? Relying on Christ to take care of his needs.

What does this passage teach us about circumstances? They change, there are good times and bad times, God is in control of the circumstances, etc.

What does it teach about contentment? That contentment depends on our attitude and our relationship with Christ, not on our circumstances.

How might this kind of contentment become real in a person's life? Through prayer and Bible study and building a relationship with the Lord.

Explain to students that if they look for contentment through a relationship with Jesus, they'll have true, lasting contentment—no matter the circumstances.

Option 2  Chat Room

You'll need Several Bibles, one poster board per group and many colorful felt-tip pens.

Have students form groups of three to five. Explain: **Today we're going to be studying part of the book of Philippians, a letter written by Paul to people who lived in a city called Philippi. But get this: Paul was in prison when he wrote it** (see

Philippians 1:13,14), **probably under house arrest in Rome** (see Acts 28:14-31). **For two years people could come and visit him, but he couldn't leave his house—ever. As you read Philippians 4:10-13, think about how you would feel if you were confined to your house.**

Give each group a poster board and several felt-tip pens. Instruct students to create movie posters advertising a movie about Paul's life, including giving the movie a title. Suggest that groups incorporate knowledge they have about Paul's life that doesn't come from Philippians 4:10-13. They could also look up other Scripture passages such as Acts 9:1-19; 27:39—28:6 and 2 Corinthians 11:24-29.

When groups have finished creating their movie posters, have them present the posters to each other; then discuss:

What are some of the circumstances Paul faced in his life as described in these passages or things you know about him? Imprisonment, blindness, healing, shipwreck, snake bite, lashed, beaten, stoned, nearly died, etc.

How do these kinds of circumstances normally affect people? They become angry or bitter, depressed, want to die, etc.

What bold claim did Paul make about how these circumstances affected him? He had learned the secret of being content in any and every situation.

How could he make such a claim? Because he had survived these difficulties with the help of Jesus.

What was the secret to Paul's contentment? His relationship with Jesus Christ.

What does it take for people to experience this kind of contentment? Prayer and Bible study and building a relationship with Jesus.

Point out to students that if they look to a relationship with Jesus for their contentment, that contentment will last—no matter the circumstances.

Option 3  Pulse Points

You'll need Several Bibles, a white board, a dry-erase marker and a package of motion sickness tablets.

The Big Idea

We can be content no matter what.

The Big Question

How is such contentment possible?

1. Only Jesus can meet our deepest needs.

Ask students to name some significant needs people have in life, such as the needs for comfort, love and security. As students call out ideas, list the needs on a white board displayed where everyone can see it.

Then ask students to name some of the ways people try to meet the kinds of needs listed. As they call out ideas, list them in a different column on the board.

Point out that these needs are very real, and only Jesus can meet our deepest needs.

2. Circumstances have no power over Jesus.

Explain: **Today we're going to be studying part of the book of Philippians, a let-**

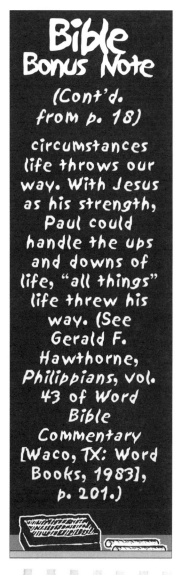

Bible Bonus Note
(Cont'd. from p. 18)

circumstances life throws our way. With Jesus as his strength, Paul could handle the ups and downs of life, "all things" life threw his way. (See Gerald F. Hawthorne, *Philippians*, vol. 43 of Word Bible Commentary [Waco, TX: Word Books, 1983], p. 201.)

Youth Leader Tip

Some groups will do better than others at creating their movie posters and capturing the big picture of what Paul's life was about. Be sure to give all the groups plenty of time to present their posters. By asking clarifying or deepening questions about their ideas, you can help to draw out Paul's story. This is a great way for junior highers to help each other learn.

ter written by Paul to people who lived in a city called Philippi. **But get this: Paul was in prison when he wrote it** (see Philippians 1:13-14), **probably under house arrest in Rome** (see Acts 28:14-31). **For two years, people could come and visit him, but he couldn't leave his house—ever.** Instruct students to think about how they would feel if they were confined to their houses as you read Philippians 4:10-12.

After reading the passage, cross items, one by one, off the list of ways people try to meet their needs. Point out that if these items are taken away or changed in our lives, our contentment will be affected if we're depending on them.

Now point to the Bible. Remind students that if our eyes are on Jesus and we're looking to Him to meet our needs, we'll be content even if these things change or are taken away.

3. True contentment comes from Jesus.

Read Philippians 4:13 and explain that students have just discovered Paul's secret: Strength to handle life's ups and downs comes from finding contentment in Jesus.

Hold up a package of motion sickness tablets and explain: **Just as these help you remain steady and comfortable on a rough ride, finding contentment in Jesus helps you remain strong and content no matter what. That doesn't mean you won't notice life's trials or experience pain but you'll have the strength you need to handle them and to remain content if your eyes are on Jesus and not on your circumstances.**

Illustrate this principle to students by sharing about a time in your own life when you experienced God's steadying strength in the midst of tough circumstances.

STEP 3 MOVING ON

This step shows students that contentment in Jesus can change lives.

Option 1 Chat Room

You'll need A TV, a VCR and the Veggie Tales video *Madame Blueberry*. (This video can be rented or purchased from most any Christian bookstore or many secular video stores.)

Ahead of time, cue the video approximately one minute and 50 seconds from opening graphic to the scene that depicts a dialogue between Bob and Larry in which Larry wishes he had more than just the new SUV; he also wishes he had the RV, the trailer and the boat.

Play the video clip; then discuss:

What was it that Larry wanted? The trailer and jet ski accessories for his new SUV.

Would Larry ever have been satisfied? No, just like us. We are never satisfied when we are looking to stuff for happiness. No matter how much we have, we will always want *more*!

Reminder

It is illegal to rent a video at the video store and show it to your youth group without first having purchased a license to do so. A blanket movie license can be bought by your church that will allow you to show virtually any movie to your youth group or congregation for one year by calling the Motion Picture Licensing Corporation at 1-800-462-8855.

How common do you think Larry's attitude is? About as common as the air we breathe.

How have you seen this attitude in people at school? Everything from the latest clothing trends to which backpack you carry to what shoes you wear.

How about in yourself? Allow personal responses from students.

If you were Bob, what would you say to him? Allow personal responses from students.

What do you think God would say to Larry? True contentment only comes from having a personal relationship with Me!

Option 2 Real Life

You'll need Copies of "Note from a Friend" (p. 23) and pens or pencils.

Distribute "Note from a Friend" and a pen or pencil to each student. Explain that the handout represents a note a friend wrote to them in study hall.

Instruct students to read the note and notice how it expresses discontentment and contentment with life. Have them pay special attention to how circumstances seem to affect their friend's sense of contentment. Then instruct students to use the backs of their handouts to write a response to the note. Have them explain what they've learned about contentment and discontentment in life.

After several minutes, ask volunteers to share what they've written.

Option 3 Tough Questions

You'll need These questions.

1. **What is contentment, anyway? How is it different than happiness?** Contentment is a sense of inner strength, peace, well-being and satisfaction that *isn't* dependent upon what's going on around us. Happiness is based on what *is* happening to us.

2. **If we're trying to allow Jesus to meet our needs, is it OK to have sad feelings sometimes?** Yes, contentment and happiness aren't the same thing. It's

OK to feel sad, but we can experience contentment in Jesus at the same time. If you feel sad a lot of the time, you might need some help from an adult to know how to really experience contentment.

3. **How is it possible to let Jesus meet our deepest needs? Where do other people fit in?** Jesus sometimes uses other people to help meet our needs. Ultimately though, our deepest needs are met through experiencing Jesus' love and peace in our lives. Then we're free to really enjoy relationships with others without demanding that they meet our needs.

4. **Is it wrong to try to improve our lives, ourselves or the circumstances of others?** No, being content doesn't mean we have to keep things as they are. Jesus wants us to make the world a better place. But we aren't dependent on these changes for our contentment.

5. **How can contentment affect our relationships with others?** When we're content, we don't look to other people to try to meet our needs. We have more to give to others. And when other people notice the contentment in our lives, they'll be attracted to Jesus.

STEP 4 — MOVING OUT

This step affirms students that only Jesus brings true contentment.

Option 1 Light the Fire

You'll need Copies of "To Be Content or Not to Be Content" (p. 24) and pens or pencils.

Distribute "To Be Content or Not to Be Content" and a pen or pencil to each student. Instruct them to work by themselves to list areas in life where they *are* content and where they are *not* content right now.

After a few minutes, discuss:

Where do you think your sense of contentment is coming from?

Where is your discontentment coming from?

What needs are you trying to meet without Jesus?

How can you draw your strength from and meet your needs in Jesus?

How would a sense of contentment change the way you live?

Ask students to circle two areas in their lives where they're not content, and write next to them something they could do to be more content in those areas. Close in prayer, asking God to help students experience life-changing contentment this week.

Option 2 Fired Up

You'll need A white board, a dry-erase marker, 3x5-inch index cards, pens or pencils and an offering plate or basket.

Ask students to name things people chase to try to bring contentment to their lives. For example, they might chase money, romance, academic success or entertainment. As students call out ideas, list them on the board.

When you've compiled a good list, instruct students to sit silently and consider these questions *without* answering out loud:

What are you personally chasing to try to bring yourself contentment?

What chase(s) do you need to give up in order to find contentment in Jesus instead?

What step can you take toward finding contentment in Jesus?

Give each student an index card and a pen or pencil. Instruct them to write on their cards things they need to stop chasing. Then take an offering for the cards. Ask students to drop their cards in an offering plate or basket to show their commitment to give up those things and find contentment in Jesus.

Option 3 Spread the Fire

You'll need Small gift boxes (or gift bags), gift wrap, transparent tape, scissors and fine-tip felt pens.

Remind students that Paul discovered the secret of being content, and it changed the way he lived. Have them silently consider these questions:

How would your life be different if you were content in Jesus, no matter what?

How would that change affect others around you?

Explain: **Your contentment can be a gift to others —showing them how Jesus can change their lives.**

Give each person a small box. Set out gift wrap, tape, scissors and fine-tip felt pens where everyone can use them. Instruct students to gift-wrap their small boxes. Then have them write on the outside of the boxes areas of their lives they need to commit to Jesus to find contentment in Him. For example, a student might write items such as "love life," "future plans" and "parents' relationship."

Point out to students that the boxes they've created represent their lives. They can be a gift to others who aren't Christians by showing true contentment in these areas of their lives. Such true contentment comes only through a relationship with Jesus.

Close with this challenge/blessing: **May you find contentment in Jesus, the only One who can meet our deepest needs. And may your life be a gift to others who don't know Jesus, showing them that He is what they're searching for.**

Have students take home their boxes to serve a reminders to be content.

NOTES

Note from a Friend

Hi,

Well, I hope your day is going better than mine. I got up late this morning and missed the bus. My mom was really mad that she had to drive me to school—I guess it makes her late to work. Then we had a pop quiz in English. We were supposed to know all these vocabulary words, but I didn't have a chance to study them. I bombed the quiz. Don't you hate it when teachers do that?

Did you know Jordan is having a party? Were you invited? I just found out about it today and I haven't gotten an invitation. I'm so mad.

I'm so excited about the dance Friday! I still can't believe I'm going with Chris. I think it will be really fun. You'll be there, right? Are you going to try to find some-one to go with you?

My parents are driving me crazy. They have this new idea that we don't spend enough time together as a family, so they're always bugging me to hang out in the living room and play games with them or something. I hate it. I hardly get to watch TV anymore. I mean, it's nice to hang out with them a little, but I need my space! What do you think I should do?

I hope I get that new stereo for my birthday. The speakers are so much better, and it has a 12-CD changer. The one I have now only holds 6. Wouldn't that be so great?

Anyway, I'll talk to you later. Don't you hate study hall? It's so boring.

Your Friend

To Be Content or Not to Be Content

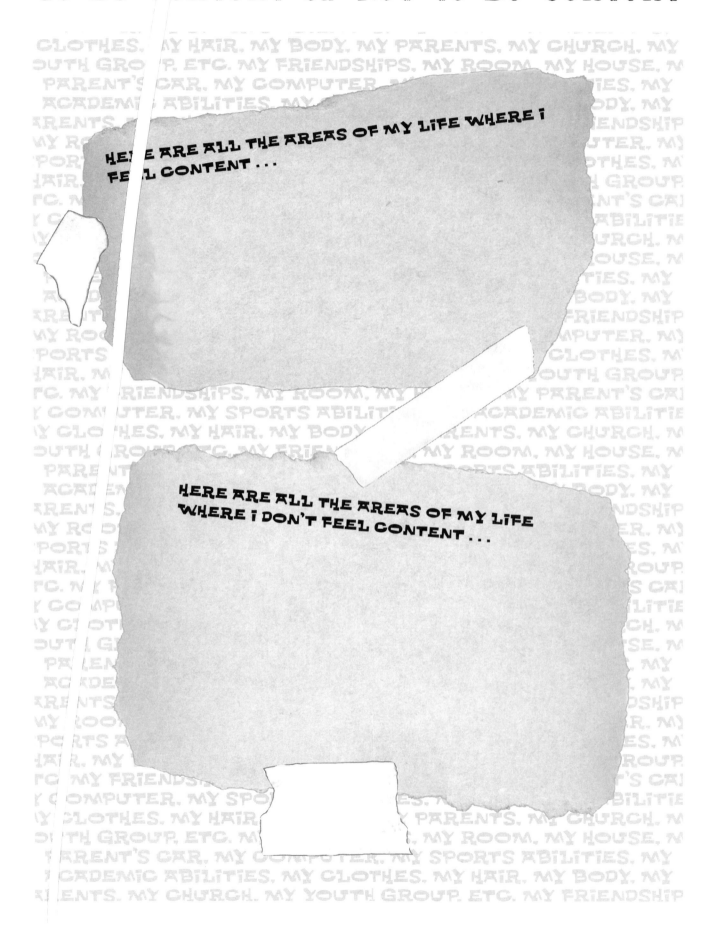

HERE ARE ALL THE AREAS OF MY LIFE WHERE I FEEL CONTENT . . .

HERE ARE ALL THE AREAS OF MY LIFE WHERE I DON'T FEEL CONTENT . . .

Devotions in Motion

FAST FACTS

Turn To Matthew 6:19-21 To read about bugs!

God Says

Suzie had her 14th birthday The day before youth group meeting. She came To The meeting wearing her new clothes, new watch and new shoes. She was so proud of her new Things That it seemed like she had a new attitude. When all of her friends confronted her about This new attitude, Suzie Thought They were jealous of all The new stuff she had. Suzie Thought That her friends would like her better because of The cool new stuff she got, so she was determined To show it off. But, boy, was she wrong.

I Do

Have you ever Thought That life would be better if you had The right shoes or The right video game? Have you ever Thought That Things would satisfy you?

What specific Things are you most Tempted To use To make you feel satisfied? How well do They work?

What have you learned about how God views stuff from Today's verse?

Pray That you can get full satisfaction from God alone Today.

FOLD HERE -

QUICK QUESTIONS

Turn To Psalm 73:25,26 and hurry!

God Says

Suppose you were going To eat only one meal for The next week. What would you choose?

- ☐ Ice cream with pickles
- ☐ Eggs with chocolate syrup
- ☐ Hot dogs and Top Ramen
- ☐ Chicken, salad and rolls

I Do

God wants To be our everything. According To Psalm 73, we will fail at Times, but God wants us To keep coming back To Him.

What does it mean To have God as your portion forever? Have you ever Thought of God as a meal That satisfies you?

What is one way you can rely on God To satisfy you Today?

Is There something you're going To have To give up or avoid in order To really know what it means To rely on God and not something or someone else? Try doing That, even if just for one day.

QUICK QUESTIONS

Do you ever feel like a loner? Then read 2 Timothy 4:16-18 to see you're not alone.

God Says

Check the boxes that apply to you.

☐ You were the last one picked for a team sport at school.

☐ You have sat alone at home all weekend.

☐ You have had plans to go somewhere with friends and they backed out.

☐ You have walked home from school alone.

I Do

How do you feel when you're lonely?

Do you ever feel like everybody else has tons of friends and you don't?

Did you know that God is always with you and can fill the void of loneliness in your life?

We often pray things such as "God, please be with me today." But get this—He already is with you today. What makes more sense is to pray that you will be aware of His presence as you go through your day. You might be surprised at how He answers this request.

FOLD HERE --

FAST FACTS

Read Mark 14:66-72. It's interesting—trust me.

God Says

It was the first day of school and Miguel had become a Christian over the summer break. He had learned about Jesus and decided to follow Him. He remembered his youth pastor talking about See You at the Pole—an event where students gather around their school flagpole to pray together. It was before school and everyone was meeting to pray, but Miguel was afraid. He thought that life was easier when he was not a Christian. Taking such a stand in front of his friends made him worry what they would think of him.

I Do

Have you ever thought that life might be easier if you were not a Christian?

Have you ever denied your faith because you were scared of what people might think of you?

As you pray today, ask God to show you how life with Him is supposed to be. Ask Him to be your strength when it is hard to be a Christian.

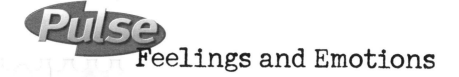

Feelings and Emotions

The Big Idea

Other kinds of love may fade away, but God's love stays with us always.

Session Aims

In this session you will guide students to:

- Understand that only God's love lasts forever;
- Experience tangible ways that God's love can change their own lives;
- Respond personally to God's love in one way this week.

The Biggest Verse

"Give thanks to the LORD, for he is good. *His love endures forever.*" Psalm 136:1 (Emphasis added)

Other Important Verses

Deuteronomy 33:27; Psalm 136; 1 John 3:16-18; 4:7-10

STEP
MOVING IN

This step helps students realize that they encounter many kinds of love.

Option 1 — Move It

You'll need Several magazines and newspapers.

Greet students and set out magazines and newspapers where everyone has access to them. Instruct students to look through the newspapers and magazines for examples of love in action—any kind of love. Examples might include love between a parent and a child, a person's love for money or possessions, dating or marriage relationships, love between people and their pets, etc. **Option:** Divide students into small groups and make it a competition to see which group can find the most examples.

As students find examples of love, have them call out descriptions of what they've found. After students have located several different examples, discuss:

If these types of love are all different, how do we know they're all love?

What do they have in common?

What makes them different?

Why are there so many kinds of love?

How many of these types of love are guaranteed to last forever?

Transition by explaining: **Today we'll take a look at the only kind of love guaranteed to last forever—God's love.**

Option 2 — Chat Room

You'll need Paper, pens or pencils, a white board and a dry-erase marker.

Greet students and have them form groups of three to five. Give each group paper and a pen or pencil. Instruct each group to come up with a definition of love. When groups have created their definitions, have them share

what they came up with. Write the definitions on the board; then help the whole group reach a consensus on *one* definition of love.

As students are working, challenge them by suggesting types of love they may not have thought to incorporate—ideas that might force them to change their definition. For example, you may remind them to consider love between family members, love between friends, love between dating or marriage partners, love between people and their pets, the love people have for money or material possessions, love for food, and so on.

When they've come up with one definition, or when they can't agree after several minutes of trying, discuss:

Why is love so hard to define? Because we use one word to describe different types of love.

Why are there so many types of love? There are many kinds of things to love.

How do we know love when we see it? People treat each other nicer, or they spend their money, time and energy on the object of their love.

When have you experienced love in your life?

Why is love so important in people's lives? Everyone needs to feel loved by at least one other person. Babies have even died due to lack of someone holding them.

Do we call some things love when they really aren't? Explain.

What kind of love do people most seem to be looking for? Romantic love.

Are some types of love more important than others? God's love, family love, friendships, marriages.

Are some longer lasting? God's love, a parent's love, some marriages.

What kinds of love are guaranteed to last forever? Only God's love.

Transition by explaining: **Today we'll take a look at the only kind of love guaranteed to last forever—God's love.**

Option 3 — Fun and Games

You'll need A stopwatch (or a watch with a seconds indicator) and candy for prizes.

Greet students and divide them into two teams to play a game of Love Charades. When the giggling over the name stops, explain the rules: A volunteer from one team will come forward and you will whisper in his or her ear a way to show love. He or she must act out what you whispered without making a sound while his or her teammates try to guess what is being acted out. Once the team has guessed the charade, you will repeat the process with the second team, and finally with additional volunteers from both teams. Be sure to explain that the actions will illustrate various kinds of love, not just one kind. Some suggestions for actions:

- Petting a dog
- A dog showing love to its master
- Eating ice cream and really enjoying it
- Caring for a child's scraped knee
- Kissing
- Playing a sport
- Proposing marriage
- Letting someone cut in line
- Giving gifts

Use the stopwatch to time how long it takes the teams to do each action. Award a candy prize to the team that guesses the most number of actions in the shortest amount of time. After the game, discuss:

Why are there so many different ways to show love? Because there are different kinds of love and what shows love to one thing or person is different, depending on the situation.

Why are there so many kinds of love? Because there are many things to love.

What kind of love do people most seem to be looking for? Romantic love.

Are some types of love more important than others? God's love, family love, friendships, marriages.

How many of these kinds of love are guaranteed to last forever? Only God's love.

Transition by explaining: **Today we'll take a look at the only kind of love guaranteed to last forever—God's love.**

This step shows that God's love lasts forever.

You'll need Several Bibles.

Explain: **Since Old Testament times, people have recognized God's amazing love by the way He acts and helps them. Psalm 136 is a long list of praises to God that**

Bible Bonus Note

Psalm 136 was written as a liturgy of praise to God. Probably a song leader led the recital of each verse, with a choir or the worshipers responding with the refrain "His love endures forever." As poetry, it follows a specific pattern: Verses 1-3 are a call to praise; vv. 4-9 tell about God's creation; vv. 10-15 about His deliverance of Israel from Egypt; v. 16 refers to the journey the Israelites made through the desert; vv. 17-22 describe the Israelites' conquest of the Promised Land. Verses 23-26 (Cont'd. on p. 30)

Youth Leader Tip

Option 1 has the potential of being either really powerful or really hokey. You know your students, so you know whether this will work with them or not. If not, we've got two additional great options for you to choose from that might fit your group better.

are based on some of the specific things God did to help His people and to reveal Himself to them.

Ask volunteers to read Psalm 136:1-26. **Option:** Have volunteers read the first part of each verse; then pause so the rest of the students can stand up and respond with the chorus: "His love endures forever."

Then ask students to share one good thing that God has done for them. If it's a guy student who shares, then all the girls should stand up when he's done and say, "His love endures forever." If it's a girl student, it's the guys' turn to stand up. Repeat this several times until students seem to run out of things to say.

Option 2  Chat Room

You'll need Several Bibles and some really mushy love cards.

Read the mushy love cards, making sure to really ham up the sappy romantic sentiments. Next, make sure each person has a Bible. Read Psalm 136 as a group, with you reading the first parts of the verses and the students reading the refrain "His love endures forever." After the reading, discuss:

Why do you think this psalm repeats the phrase "His love endures forever" so many times? It was a way of reminding people what God has done for them and worshiping Him. It's like the chorus of a worship song, repeated so that we remember.

What kinds of evidence of God's love is included in this psalm? His creation, deliverance, protection, gifts, etc.

What kind of evidence of God's love have you seen in your own life?

How can God's love last forever? Because He is infinite; He is eternal, etc.

What makes God's love different from other kinds of love? Because it is unconditional and eternal.

How does this passage illustrate the eternal nature of God's love? By describing what He has done from the beginning of creation through the ages.

Why should we believe God's promise that His love lasts forever? Because He sent His only Son to die for our sins, even before we were born.

What is God's love based on? His character, which is constant, never-changing.

How does God show His love? In so many ways, such as sending His Son to die for us, creating us, always keeping His promises, etc.

How can knowing that God's love lasts forever change our lives? It gives us security not only in this present life but also after we die. We should live in a way that expresses that security, sharing God's love with everyone and not living fearfully or timidly.

Option 3  Pulse Points

You'll need Several Bibles, a large piece of paper, a felt-tip pen, a watch, a white board and a dry-erase marker.

Ahead of time, create a contract on a large piece of paper. This will serve as a prop for point 2. The contract should simply say, "I promise to love you forever. God."

The Big Idea

God's love lasts forever.

The Big Question

How do we know God's love lasts forever?

1. God is forever.

Explain: **God can love us forever because God *is* forever. He always has existed and always will. He never changes. He created time. He created everything!**

Read Deuteronomy 33:27. Hold up the watch so that everyone can see it and continue: **Isn't it comforting to know that God doesn't wear a watch? We're at the mercy of time, always. But God never is. He was the same 1,000 years ago as He is right now. And He'll be the same for you today as He is tomorrow.**

2. God keeps His promises.

Read Psalm 136. Emphasize: **God has shown His love to people since the beginning of time, and He won't ever stop. He keeps His promises, just as He did for the people of Israel in the ways described in this passage.**

Display the contract you created beforehand. Continue: **It's as if God has signed a contract and will never break His word to us.**

3. God is love.

Write "Love is . . ." on the white board and have students call out a few quick one- or two-word definitions. As they do so, write the definitions below the sentence starter.

Read 1 John 4:7-10 and explain: **God invented love and continues to show us what love is. God's nature ultimately shows us what love is. The ultimate act of love was Jesus' death on our behalf.** Write "God" across the students' list of definitions.

NOTES

STEP **3** MOVING ON

This step examines how God's love can change our lives.

Option 1 Chat Room

You'll need Copies of "Love Letter from God" (p. 35).

Distribute "Love Letter from God" and ask students to read their handouts silently. Allow a few moments for reading; then discuss:

How does this letter make you feel?

Did anything in this letter surprise you?

Why do you think God loves us? Because He is God and He created us.

How does God show His love to people? By taking care of them, by sending His only Son to die for them, etc.

How have you experienced God's love in your life?

How did this love letter compare to a love letter you might get from another person?

What are some of the things that make God's love different from other kinds of love? It is unconditional and eternal.

How does God's love change people's lives?

How can you experience God's love more fully? By spending more time with Him in prayer and Bible study.

How does God want us to respond to His love? By accepting His love, worshiping Him, putting Him first in our lives, etc.

How can we write "love letters" to God? By keeping a prayer journal and by telling others about His love.

Option 2 Real Life

You'll need The following case study. Oh yeah, and you'll also need to have a good time with your students today!

Share the following case study:

I just don't get this love stuff. My dad tells me that he loves me, but then he's so busy with work that

I never get to see him. Last Wednesday he promised he'd come to my soccer game, but he missed it—again. And when he does show up, he's usually late. Plus, he has that stupid cell phone that rings all the time. So right in the middle of a cool conversation with him, he gets distracted.

And then my boyfriend used to tell me that he loved me too. But come to think of it, he only said it if I said it first. Since he broke up with me last Thursday, I wonder if he really meant it at all. Maybe he was just saying that because he felt like it was what I wanted to hear or I might break up with him.

And now at church they're talking about God's love. Yeah, right. It's probably no different than my dad or my boyfriend. God is probably too busy for me or is going to break up with me too.

Discuss:

What would you say to this person?

How do you think she is feeling? Lonely, betrayed, etc.

Do you think her feelings are common to girls? Why?

How about for guys? Do they have the same feelings?

Given what we learned from Psalm 136, what would you tell this person about God's love?

Option 3 Tough Questions

You'll need Just these questions.

1. **Is it OK to love other people and things besides God?** Yes, God wants us to love other people and take joy in the blessings He gives us. But these things should never get in the way of our love for God.

2. **Does God love some people more than others?** No. God loves everyone equally. Even though it may seem like God should love Christians more than non-Christians, He doesn't. And although some people have more possessions and advantages in life, it's important to remember that these things aren't indicators of how much God does or doesn't love us. Christ died for everyone. That's the ultimate display of His love.

3. **If God's love lasts forever, why does the world seem to be getting worse?** Because God loves us, He allows us to make our own choices. As people choose to disobey God, the world suffers the consequences of sin. The more time passes, the more the consequences of sin pile up for the world. In addition, Satan is God's enemy who opposes God's plan. Satan uses lies and deceptions to cause trouble in this world.

4. **If God loves people so much, why is there so much suffering?** Suffering comes as a result of living in an imperfect world. Because people have chosen to disobey God, the world is no longer perfect and we live with the consequences of sin. God shows His love to people who are suffering, even though He doesn't always stop the suffering. God's love makes it possible for His followers to leave this world someday and live in perfection—heaven—with Him.

STEP MOVING OUT

This step establishes that we all must respond to God's love—and that we can do it right now!

Option 1 Light the Fire

You'll need A white board, a dry-erase marker, a CD (or cassette) of worship music and a CD (or cassette) player.

Draw a large heart on the white board and summarize: **God has extended His love to us and now we must decide what we will do about it—either accept it or reject it. Maybe you accepted God's love at one time, but lately you've been pushing it away by doing your own thing. Or maybe you've never accepted God's love. If that's the case, I want to explain something to you. Refusing to let go of sin blocks us from experiencing God's love. God sent His Son, Jesus, to demolish that obstacle of sin and give you the way to have a relationship with Him again. The way has been made! When you give your life to Jesus, sin is taken out of the** way so that you can enjoy an awesome awareness of God's love and presence in your life.

Instruct students to spread out in the room so everyone has some privacy. Play the worship music and have students think about accepting God's love or renewing their commitment to God. Encourage them to spend some time talking to God about the commitment they'd like to make.

After several minutes, invite students who want to make a commitment to write their names in the heart. Be sure students know that if they aren't ready to make commitments, that's OK.

Invite students to talk to you afterward if they'd like to discuss the commitments they've made. Whether or not students talk with you, follow up by calling or e-mailing those who wrote their names on the heart. When you contact them, ask whether or not they'd like to talk about their commitments. If they say no, assure them that it's OK and that you're praying for them.

Option 2 — Fired Up

You'll need A clear water pitcher filled with water and two clear glasses.

Explain: **One of the major things that separates Christianity from all other religions is the unconditional way God loves us. Even though our sin made us guilty before Him, He sent His Son, Jesus, to make a way for us to have relationship with Him again.**

And now that we know His love and have that relationship, we have a new motivation to serve God and others. Unlike other religions, we don't serve God and others to earn His favor or to rack up points in heaven. We do it because it is a natural outflow of the love of God that we've experienced.

Demonstrate this by using the water pitcher and glasses. Explain: **God is like this water pitcher. When He pours His love** (pour water from the pitcher into the first glass) **into you, then you can share that love with someone else** (pour water from the first glass into the second glass).

Give students a few minutes alone to think about the way that they're sharing God's love with others. Are they aware of God's love? If so, are they sharing that with others in tangible ways?

If you have time, bring the whole group back together and ask them to share some of the ways they realized that they were sharing God's love with others in tangible ways. Invite students to come up with one new way to show God's love to someone this week—maybe even someone hard to love, like a sibling or a person at school that no one likes—but someone who needs God's love just the same!

NOTES

Youth Leader Tip

Before this activity, ask some other adults to be ready to talk with students who want to discuss their commitments. Let them know what you'll be talking about and provide some training on listening, counseling and leading someone to Christ. Ask these adults to be available at the end of the session or to help you follow up with students later.

Option 3

Spread the Fire

You'll need Your Bible, paper and pens or pencils.

Point out that God's love demands a response. If we've already responded by accepting it, then God wants us to show His love to others.

Read 1 John 3:16-18. Summarize: **Once we've experienced God's love, He wants us to love others the same way. This is not easy most of the time, but God does help us love others as He loves us.**

Give each student paper and a pen or pencil. Ask them to think of someone who needs to know about God's love. Instruct students to write "God's love letter" to that person. The letter should be written from God's perspective to the person who needs to know about God's love, expressing how much God loves that person.

When students have finished their letters, encourage them to follow through either by giving the person the letter or by telling the person about God's love in some other way. Close in prayer, asking God to give students the opportunities and strength they need to follow through.

NOTES

Love Letter from God

Dear Child,

I'm writing to tell you how much I love you. I know I told you yesterday, and every day before that, but I can't let a day go by without reminding you of my love.

When I look at you, I can't help but remember creating you. I remember putting together all the different parts of your body, guiding the process of cells dividing, putting on the finishing touches that make you the individual you are. You turned out beautifully!

I love watching you grow and change, becoming a more mature person. I also love placing opportunities in your life, so you can develop as a person. I've given you so many gifts and talents, and it's so fun to see you use them!

I don't need anything from you. I love you and I don't expect anything in return. I love you because I choose to love you, and I want you to have a relationship with me because you need me.

I know it's easy for you to get bogged down in the everyday concerns of life, but you'll have so much more joy if you look for evidence of my love in your life every day. I show my love in so many ways: the sunrise, the sunset, the smile on a stranger's face, the gift of music, your heartbeat, your relationships—so many ways. And I love to hear you respond to my love in worship.

In the busyness of your daily life, don't forget about my love for you. If you accept my love, it will bring you so much joy and peace. And you'll have so much love to give away to others.

Love,
God

Devotions in Motion

WEEK TWO: LOVE

DAY 1

QUICK QUESTIONS

Can you ever lose God's love? Read Romans 8:35-39 for the answer.

God Says

Which circumstance would make it hard for you to love your friends?

☐ Your friend spreads rumors about you all over school

☐ Your friend steals money from you.

☐ Your friend borrows a CD and breaks it.

☐ Your friend buys you a present.

I Do

Have you ever thought that God could stop loving you? What have you learned from these verses in Romans?

When you do something bad, God continues to love you. There is nothing you can do to make Him not love you. How would your life be different if you really, really, really knew that God loved you all the time?

FOLD HERE -

DAY 4

FAST FACTS

Read John 3:16 and read about true love.

God Says

Angela invited her friend Jenny to come to church. During the sermon, the pastor talked about things we might love more than God. After church, Jenny asked to borrow some of Angela's favorite CDs. Angela was so attached to her CDs that it was hard to give them up to Jenny. But she remembered what her pastor said and, although it was hard, she loaned her CDs to Jenny.

I Do

Have you ever felt like Angela and found it hard to give up some of your things to other people? What kinds of things were they?

What do you think it was like for God to give His only Son to die for the world?

Remember today how much God loves people—so much that He would send Jesus to die on a cross for us. Are you willing to give up things to love people too, just as God did in sending His Son, Jesus, for us?

DAY 2

FAST FACTS

Read Hebrews 13:5. You will dig it!

God Says

Sam is 12 years old. His father left his mom and him a year ago, which has made Sam question whether or not his dad even loved him in the first place. In the past year, Sam has also had three really close friends move away. Plus his older brother left for college. Sam is having trouble understanding that God will never leave him. What would you tell Sam?

I Do.

Have you known people who have left or moved away? Do you miss them?

What have you learned about God from the verse you read today?

Isn't it encouraging to know that God is ALWAYS with you? Spend three minutes right now telling God how thankful you are that He will never leave you.

FOLD HERE ------

DAY 3

QUICK QUESTIONS

Ever been scared? Read Isaiah 41:10.

God Says

Rate these situations from the scariest (4) to the least scary (1).

___ Hearing noises while you are camping with your family

___ Seeing a Great Dane run toward you

___ Watching a scary movie on television

___ Seeing your science teacher in public

I Do.

God loves us so much that we do not need to be scared. Although being scared is a natural feeling, God's love can overpower our feelings of being afraid.

Are there things in your life that you are scared about? Tell God today about those things right now and ask for His love to overpower them!

SESSIONTHREESESSIONTHREESESSIONTHREE

The Big Idea

God's acceptance of us shows us how we should accept others.

Session Aims

In this session you will guide students to:

- Understand why God wants them to accept others;
- Experience how God has accepted them;
- Commit to one specific way to accept others as God has accepted them this week.

The Biggest Verse

"Accept one another, then, just as Christ accepted you, in order to bring praise to God." Romans 15:7

Other Important Verses

John 15:14,15; Romans 5:6-8; 14:1—15:13; 1 John 1:9

Acceptance

STEP

MOVING IN

This step reminds students that everyone needs acceptance.

Option 1  Move It

You'll need Paper, a pen or pencil and masking tape.

Ahead of time, create several short character profiles and write them on pieces of paper. Each profile should include a brief description of the person and his or her characteristics. Make some of them positive and others negative. For example, you might describe a serial killer on one piece of paper, a suburban mom on another piece of paper, a gossipy teenager on another and a church pastor on another. You'll need one profile for each student.

Greet students and tape a profile on each person's back. Be sure they can't see the profile on their own backs. Instruct students to walk around the room, reading the profiles on each other's backs. They should start conversations with each other, treating each other according to their profiles. Instruct students not to tell each other what's on their backs, but to give clues by treating them in certain ways. As students talk with others, they should try to guess what profiles they've been assigned. If a guess is incorrect, simply tell the person to keep participating and trying to figure out the profile. If the guess is correct, tell the person to continue giving clues to others. After several minutes of this activity, discuss:

If you guessed your profile, how did you figure it out?

If you didn't guess your profile, what would have helped you figure it out?

In this activity, how did you communicate acceptance or rejection to others?

How did this activity compare to the ways we accept or reject each other in real life?

Why is it so important for people to feel accepted? We need to feel a part of society; we would be lonely without acceptance of others, etc.

Explain: Everyone needs acceptance, and as we'll see today, we face all sorts of important choices every day to accept or reject other people.

Option 2  Chat Room

You'll need Paper, scissors, a felt-tip pen, chairs, a hat or box and a treat everyone can enjoy (candy, cookies, etc.).

Ahead of time, cut paper into small slips, one slip for each person. Mark one third of the slips of paper, with a star (or any similar symbol) and leave the rest blank. Fold all the slips of paper and put them in a hat or box. Set up the same number of chairs as you have slips of marked paper.

Greet students and have them each draw a folded slip of paper from the hat or box and remain standing. Ask: **How many of you have a star on your paper?** Invite students that have marks on their papers to sit down and enjoy a treat; everyone else must stand and watch.

After a few minutes, let everyone else pull out chairs, sit and eat too; then discuss:

How did it feel to be accepted into a chair and be given a treat?

How did it feel to be rejected?

How was this activity like acceptance and rejection in real life?

When have you experienced acceptance in real life? How did it feel?

When have you experienced rejection in real life? How did it feel?

What are some things people accept or reject others for in real life? Looks, intelligence, position, money, age, etc.

How do people show acceptance in real life? By being friendly, by talking nicely to the person, by smiling at a person, etc.

How do people show rejection in real life? By ignoring them, by calling them names, by pushing them out of the way, by laughing at them, etc.

What do people do to try to get acceptance? Give gifts to people, do or say things to attract attention, follow the leader in a group, etc.

Why is it so important for people to feel accepted? It is an important need for us all to feel accepted by at least someone.

Transition to the rest of the lesson by explaining: **As we'll see today, we face all sorts of choices every day about whether or not to accept or reject people.**

Option 3  Fun and Games

You'll need One chair per student.

Ahead of time, set up the chairs in a circle, facing inward.

Greet students with wild enthusiasm and invite them to take a seat. Stand in the center of the circle and explain that you're going to call out a particular feature or characteristic that students might have in common with you, such as wearing tennis shoes or has blue eyes. Students who have the feature you name are to stand up and trade seats with each other. This is when you're going to try to grab a seat for yourself. Whoever is left without a seat will take his or her place in the middle of the circle and must call out the next characteristic or feature.

Play the game for several rounds; then discuss:

In this game how did you decide what to call out?

How was this game similar to the ways we choose to accept or reject other people in real life? We look on the outside appearance, not on who they really are on the inside.

How does it feel to be accepted?

How does it feel to be rejected?

Why is acceptance so important to people? It is an important need for us all to feel accepted by at least someone.

Transition to the rest of the lesson by explaining: **Just like this game, we often judge people based on whether or not they are like us, but as we'll see today, God wants us to act differently than this. He wants us to accept others.**

STEP 2 MOVING UP

This step shows how God accepts us.

Option 1  Move It

You'll need Your Bible, board games, video game systems and other things for students to do together for 10 minutes without any supervision.

Ahead of time, find a junior higher who your students don't know and ask him or her to come to your meeting. Ask the volunteer to dress kinda nerdy—maybe not even brush his or hair that whole day. Instruct the volunteer to stand far away from the others and not talk to anyone, unless someone talks to him or her first.

Explain that you want to give students 10 minutes just to hang out and have fun, and point out everything you've brought that they can do. Make sure you have enough

Bible Bonus Note

The church in Rome had a particular struggle with accepting one another. This is because the church consisted of Gentiles and Jews, who each had different perspectives on what it meant to be a Christian. Some of the Jewish people believed Gentiles should conform to Jewish standards of behavior as part of becoming Christians. Some Gentiles felt that they didn't need to follow the Jewish laws. Because the issue of acceptance was such a hot one in the Roman church, Paul included an (Cont'd. on p. 42)

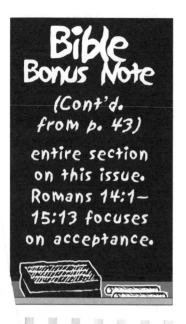

Bible Bonus Note

(Cont'd. from p. 43)

entire section on this issue. Romans 14:1–15:13 focuses on acceptance.

adults around so that students have some supervision, but at the same time, let them run around and get rid of some energy.

After 10 minutes, call the group back together. Introduce the junior higher who stood on the outskirts of the group and ask him or her:

Did anybody talk to you?

How did you feel standing there?

What do you think they thought of you?

Ask the rest of the group:

How many of you even noticed this student?

For those of you who noticed, what did you think of our visitor?

What kept you from talking to this new person?

For those of you who talked to the newcomer, what motivated you to do so?

Explain: **We often feel like we have to know somebody first, and that the person has to act or dress a certain way before we accept him or her. God is much different than that.**

Read Romans 5:8 and discuss: **What does this say about God's acceptance of us?**

Read Romans 5:6,7 and discuss:

What did it cost God to accept us? The suffering and death of His only Son.

What would it cost you to accept other people, even people you don't know or who aren't cool? My "cool" reputation might be damaged; my pride might be hurt; others might laugh at me; etc.

Option 2  Chat Room

You'll need Several Bibles, a white board and a dry-erase marker. **Note:** You might also want to make copies of the small-group questions for this option, so students won't have to strain to remember them (and drive you crazy asking you to repeat them every 14 seconds).

Ask students to help you make two lists: one list of words to describe God and one list of words to describe people. As students call out ideas, make the lists in two columns on the white board.

When the lists are complete, ask students to compare the two lists. Explain: **Looking at these two lists, it's easy to see how ridiculous it is that people should expect anything from God, least of all love and acceptance. Why should God accept us, considering who we are and who He is?**

Have students form small groups. Distribute Bibles and assign each group one of the following Scripture passages: Romans 5:8; 1 John 1:9 or John 15:14,15. Instruct groups to read their assigned Scripture and to discuss the following questions in their groups:

How does this passage show God's acceptance of us?

How can this kind of acceptance affect a person's life?

Why is it important to know that God accepts us in this way?

If groups are struggling, you can give them the following pointers: Romans 5:8 shows the incredible love of God for completely undeserving people. He gave us the greatest gift He could—His life—even before we realized that we needed it! In John 15:14,15, Jesus makes the amazing statement that although He is the Son of God, He is a friend to others; they aren't just His servants, they also have a relationship with

Him. In 1 John 1:9, we learn that God is faithful and just to forgive us and accept us, even when we really blow it.

After several minutes of discussion, have groups summarize for each other what they discovered. Discuss:

Why do you think God has chosen to accept us in these ways?

How does it feel to know that God accepts us?

How have you been affected by God's acceptance?

Which of these three ways has affected your life the most?

Have you heard of someone else being affected by God's acceptance? How were they affected?

Why is it important to know how God accepts us? Because the rest of the world is not always accepting, but He loves and accepts us as we are.

What's so amazing about God's acceptance? That He knows us better than anyone—the good and the bad—and He still loves us.

How should we respond to God's acceptance? We should want to get to know Him better and show His love and acceptance to others.

Summarize: **If God has accepted us in Christ, how can we reject others? God is far superior to us and has no reason to accept us—except for His love. We're no better than anyone else and yet we reject each other all the time. If God accepts us, we should accept others.**

Option 3  Pulse Points

You'll need Your Bible, a paper bag, an unusual but edible food item (such as a jar of baby food, a mango, a block of tofu, etc.), an overhead projector, a picture of you that has been photocopied onto a transparency, a blank transparency, a transparency marker and a screen or blank wall.

Ahead of time, place the food item in the paper bag.

The Big Idea
God accepts us.

The Big Question
How does God show His acceptance of us?

1. God loves us just as we are.
Read Romans 5:8 and explain: **God showed His love by sending Jesus to die in our place—even though we**

hadn't done anything for Him or even tried to change our ways. We've all broken God's laws and deserve punishment. God has never owed us anything. But God took the punishment for our sin before we even admitted we were wrong.

Hold up the paper bag with the food in it. Offer it to anyone who will promise to eat the entire thing without knowing what's in the bag. If someone volunteers, give the person the bag. Point out that this is somewhat similar to what God has done for us—Christ gave up His life for us without waiting first to see whether we would accept Him or change our ways.

2. God forgives us.
Read 1 John 1:9 and explain: **We all sin—we do things that break God's laws. When we sin, it forms a barrier between us and God.**

On an overhead projector, display a picture of you with a clear transparency over it. Ask students to name some common sins people commit. As they call out ideas, write them on the clear transparency, so they cover the picture of you.

Continue: **When God forgives us, He no longer sees the sins when He looks at us.** Pull the clear transparency away to reveal the clear picture of you again.

3. God wants us to have a relationship with Him.
Read John 15:14,15. Explain: **God actually calls His followers** *friends*! **We can be friends with God because He accepts us.**

Ask students to describe how people decide where to sit at lunch at school. Allow for a few responses; then continue: **It's like God is the most popular person at school and we're all invited to sit at His lunch table!**

Summarize: **If God accepts us, then how can we reject others? God is far superior to us and has no reason to accept us—except for His love. We're no better than anyone else and yet we reject each other all the time.** Read Romans 15:7 and conclude: **If God accepts us, we should accept others.**

NOTES

STEP 3
MOVING ON

This step points out that God wants us to accept others.

Option 1  Chat Room

You'll need A white board and a dry erase marker.

Begin by asking: **How do people show rejection?** As students call out ideas, list them on the white board.

Discuss: **What would happen to our group if we stopped doing these things to each other? What keeps us from accepting others?**

Transition to the next idea by asking: **What are some specific ways people communicate acceptance?** As students call out ideas, write them next to the list of ways people show rejection. Discuss:

What would happen if we did these things in this group every time we got together?

What if we did these things all the time, everywhere we went?

How would the world be different if everyone accepted everyone? It would be a lot friendlier, no wars, no gangs, no killing.

How would people feel about God if Christians were more accepting toward each other? They would probably be more interested in learning about God.

What would happen if Christians were more accepting toward non-Christians? That would really get everyone's attention! The world would be dramatically changed.

What keeps us from communicating acceptance all the time? We think only of ourselves; our relationship with God slips due to sin or not spending time with Him.

Why do you think God wants us to accept others? So that we can show His love to everyone; because He loves us.

What can we do to come closer to accepting everyone? Focus on what Jesus did for us and how much God loves us and everyone else.

Option 2  Real Life

You'll need A video camera, a blank videotape, a TV, a VCR and access to a group of junior highers besides your own. **Option:** Use an audiocassette recorder and audiocassette to record the interviews.

Ahead of time, videotape (or record on audiocassette) interviews with real junior highers, asking them the following questions: **When have you experienced acceptance? When is it hard for you to accept others? Who is hard for you to accept?**

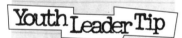

Youth Leader Tip

To get the interviews for this activity, try visiting another youth group. Call another youth worker beforehand and get permission to visit and record the interviews with junior highers before, during or after their meeting. Other youth groups are a great place to find several junior highers all in one place, and they're in a setting where they're usually willing to talk about important life issues.

Play the tape of the interviews you recorded earlier. After the interviews, discuss:

How does acceptance affect someone's life? It can make the difference between having a happy productive life or having a lonely, difficult life.

What makes it hard to accept some people? Some people are different from you, or they are weird or they make it hard to accept them by being angry or mean.

Why do you think God wants us to accept others? To reflect His love for them.

If God has accepted us, why does that mean we should accept others? He has told us to!

How can we become more accepting? By following Jesus' example.

You'll need Nothing, 'cept the questions below.

1. **Does accepting others mean we let them walk all over us?** No. Accepting others means not trying to change them or push them away because of who they are or the way they act. That doesn't mean we shouldn't protect ourselves or respectfully avoid people who mistreat us.

2. **Does accepting others mean we pretend they're perfect?** No. Accepting others doesn't mean we have to pretend they have no faults. In fact, the highest form of acceptance is to acknowledge that a person isn't perfect, yet we should love and accept that person anyway. Remember, we *all* have faults.

3. **Why should we accept people who don't accept us?** God accepts us, even when we reject Him. Remember, Christ gave up His life for us without even waiting for us to change our ways. Our acceptance shouldn't be based on other people's behavior but on a response to God's acceptance of us. However, if someone continues to reject you, maybe you should talk to a Christian adult and get his or her advice about how best to respond.

4. **Why does God care how we treat other people?** God loves and cares about everyone. He hates to see us mistreat each other. He wants us to show His love to each other. Most times people get their best glimpses of God through those who follow Him.

This step presents a challenge to accept others as God accepts us right now.

You'll need Nada. Zippo. Nothing.

Have students sit quietly, perhaps closing their eyes or covering their faces. Ask them to think of someone they've been rejecting, either actively or passively. Pause for a few moments, then ask students to think of at least one specific way they can commit to communicating God's acceptance and their own acceptance to that person.

After a few moments, ask students to form pairs. Instruct them to share with their partners the accepting actions they came up with. Partners should then pray for each other to follow through on their commitments. **Note:** Be sure to ask students to talk about their commitments without revealing the names of the people they've been rejecting.

You'll need Copies of "Acceptance Commitment" (p. 47) and pens or pencils.

Have students spread out around the room. Distribute "Acceptance Commitment" and a pen or pencil to each student. Instruct them to spend some time in prayer, asking God to bring to their minds the names of people they need to accept. Then they should complete the handout with the names that came to mind. They may fill in all the lines with the same name or put a different name on each line. They may even put more than one name on each line.

When students are finished with their handouts, close in prayer, asking God to help students follow through on their commitments.

Encourage students to take their handouts home as reminders of their commitments.

Option 3  Spread the Fire

You'll need Just some willing students.

Explain: **The way we accept people tells them a lot about the kind of people we are. Since we are followers of Jesus, the way we accept people can tell them a lot about the God that we serve.**

Ask students to think of one common situation in which a junior higher gets rejected; then have two volunteers come forward. One volunteer is the student being rejected and the second is a Christian student. Have the volunteers begin a conversation about the situation, assuming that the Christian student knows what has happened. Encourage the audience to pay attention. Whenever they want to jump in, all they have to do is yell "Freeze," at which point the two volunteers stop. The person who yelled "Freeze," then walks up and takes the place of one of the students (he or she get to choose) and completes the action the way he or she would do it. Continue this until someone else yells "Freeze," or until the conversation starts to hit a dead end. If you have time, repeat this with additional situations and volunteers.

Give students a few minutes to pray on their own, thinking about people that they know who don't know Jesus and are hungry to feel accepted. Challenge students to do something this week to let those people know that they are accepted. Who knows? Maybe they'll get curious about the God who accepts them too!

Acceptance Commitment

Because God loves me as I am, I will love _____ just as he or she is.

Because God forgives me, I will forgive _____.

Because God considers me a friend, I will treat _____ as a friend.

Signed _____ Date _____

Acceptance Commitment

Because God loves me as I am, I will love _____ just as he or she is.

Because God forgives me, I will forgive _____.

Because God considers me a friend, I will treat _____ as a friend.

Signed _____ Date _____

Devotions in Motion

WEEK THREE: ACCEPTANCE

DAY 1

FAST FACTS

If you like numbers, go to Matthew 18:21,22.

God Says

Jordan and Ryan were best friends. Then Ryan lied to Jordan, which made Jordan feel really hurt. Ryan asked Jordan for forgiveness, but Jordan was still hurt and stayed mad at him for several days. The next Sunday his junior high youth leader talked about Matthew 18:21,22. When Jordan saw Ryan the following day in school, he remembered that we are supposed to forgive one another because God commands us to. It was not easy to do, but Jordan forgave Ryan.

I Do

Forgiveness might not be easy, but it is what we are called to do. Has it ever been hard for you to forgive someone?

Can you think of some people in your life you need to forgive? Ask God to give you strength to forgive them soon, like maybe even today.

FOLD HERE ---

DAY 4

QUICK QUESTIONS

Need some help? Read Galatians 6:2.

God Says

What could you do to help these people?

Mario's parents just got a divorce.

  I could _____

Amy broke her leg.

  I could _____

Renaldo lost the championship soccer game.

  I could _____

Mom burned your best shirt while ironing it.

  I could _____

I Do

Have you ever felt like you wanted to help someone but you didn't know how? We can be the biggest help to people by simply asking what we can do to help them out. Or we can ask God to help us think of a way to help them.

Write down the names of two people who you can ask to help this week.

  I could offer to help _____ and _____

Now do it! It does you no good to just write it down so go do it now! Hurry!

QUICK QUESTIONS

DAY 2

Ever been really mad at someone? Read Ephesians 4:31,32 To see whaT To do.

God Says

Place an A beside Those ThaT display anger and a K beside Those ThaT show kindness.

____ Having a Temper TanTrum

____ WriTing a noTe To encourage your parenTs

____ Asking how your friend is feeling

____ Cussing aT somebody

I Do.

SomeTimes when we are angry, iT is hard To be kind. According To The verse you read Today, whaT does God wanT us To do?

WhaT are Two specific Things ThaT you can do Today To be kind and compassionaTe To people you come in conTacT wiTh?

FOLD HERE

FAST FACTS

DAY 3

Turn To Mark 12:28-33—if you dare!

God Says

Everybody aT church Thinks Judy has an on-fire relaTionship wiTh Jesus. She is The firsT To youTh group and The firsT To Sunday School. She is The firsT To sign up for camp. She knows all The answers all The Time. BuT when Judy geTs To school, she is differenT. She doesn'T Talk To anyone who is noT a ChrisTian. She never inviTes anyone To church. In facT, she is preTTy isolaTed aT school. She says she does noT have Time To Talk To people because her church acTiviTies are more imporTanT.

I Do.

WhaT is wrong wiTh Judy's relaTionship wiTh God?

God says ThaT we need To firsT love Him and Then love oTher people. Who are The unlovable people in your life?

WhaT are Three specific Things ThaT you can do Today To be ChrisTlike To Those people?

Ask God To help you do Those Things Today.

50

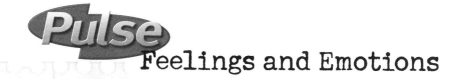

Feelings and Emotions

The Big Idea

We can lose everything else, but God will never abandon us.

Session Aims

In this session you will guide students to:

- Learn that God will never abandon them, even when they don't recognize His presence;
- Experience the temporary nature of things and people around us;
- Respond by placing their trust in God, not the world around us.

The Biggest Verse

"My ears had heard of you but now my eyes have seen you."
Job 42:5

Other Important Verses

Job 1—2; 38; 42:1-17

STEP
MOVING IN

This step helps students reflect on how it feels to lose something or someone important.

Option 1  Move It

You'll need Several sheets of red, blue, yellow and green paper, scissors, envelopes (one for each student), poster board and a felt-tip pen (or a white board and a dry-erase marker).

Ahead of time, cut the paper into small slips. Put six slips of paper (in any combination of colors) in each envelope, making sure you have one envelope prepared for each student. Also, make a chart using the following information:

- Blue takes red
- Red takes yellow
- Yellow takes green and blue
- Green takes red

Greet students and give each one an envelope with the slips of paper inside. Point out the chart and instruct students to begin a paper war. Here's how it works: When two people meet, each one must reveal one slip of paper. Depending on the colors of the two slips of paper, one person takes both slips of paper—the other person must willingly surrender the losing slip of paper.

Have students play for several minutes. If students run out of papers, have them sit down until you call time.

After several minutes, stop the activity and take inventory of how their paper collections have changed. Find out who completely ran out of papers, who ended up with the most, etc.

Discuss:

How was this activity like losing people and things in real life?

How is it different?

How does losing something or someone important change our lives? It leaves an empty spot in our lives. It might even cause big changes to lose something or someone such as your home or a loved one who dies.

Why do some people end up suffering more loss than others? It might depend on the importance of what they lost or difficulties caused by the loss. Some people just take things harder.

How do people deal with loss? Many ways: anger, bitterness, withdrawing, running away, crying a lot, praying, etc.

Point out: **It's never easy to lose someone or something important to you. We can't count on anything in life staying the same or always being around. But as we'll see today, we can count on God. He'll never abandon us.**

Option 2  Chat Room

You'll need Nothing but these questions.

Greet students and have them form two equal circles, one standing inside the other. The students forming the outer circle should face in and the students in the inner circle should face out. Each person should be facing someone in the other circle. If you're short a person in either circle, join that circle to make up the difference.

Instruct students that you'll be posing some questions to them. Students should discuss each question with the person they're facing, then rotate after each question with the inner circle rotating counterclockwise and the outer circle moving clockwise. Discuss:

When have you lost some*thing* important to you? How did that feel?

When have you lost some*one* important to you? How did that feel?

How have you dealt with losing important people or things in your life?

What are some things people do to try to avoid experiencing loss?

Ask students to return to their seats, and continue to discuss:

What kinds of things make us feel a sense of loss in our lives? Moving away, changing schools, parents' divorcing, death of someone, a friend who suddenly decides not to be your friend, having something stolen or broken, etc.

Why is loss such a big part of life? Because life is always changing, nothing stays the same.

What would we have to do to truly avoid experiencing loss? Not have any relationships or possessions, not make any connections, etc.

How does losing something or someone important affect our lives? It hurts, feels lonely, makes us want to not be connected to anything or anyone, etc.

How does the pain of loss change as we grow older? Our losses might be bigger. We will experience even more loss, but we might learn how to better handle it.

What makes some losses more painful than others? The connections are stronger to some people than to others, such as someone you see every day. The importance of a thing to your life, such as the loss of your home, is more painful than the loss of a favorite toy.

What makes some people handle loss better than others? Having a support group, family and friends to comfort us, knowing Jesus.

What are some ways to deal with significant loss? Pray, cry, talk with friends or family or other adults, serve others in need, etc.

Explain: **We've all experienced loss in some way. Loss is always painful, and it always changes our lives. We can't count on anything or anyone on earth to always be there. But as we'll see today, God will always be there.**

Option 3  Fun and Games

You'll need A bunch of balloons and a volleyball net (or a piece of rope).

Ahead of time, fill the balloons with air and string the net (or rope) between two secure objects, each approximately five to six feet off of the ground. Make sure to tie it securely to each object. **Option:** Arrange to have two volunteers hold the net.

Greet students, divide them into two teams and let them know that they are going to play a game of balloon volleyball. They are to play using the same rules as regular volleyball—with one catch. Periodically, you will call out different instructions for teams to follow as they play. Explain that once you give a command to a team, members must follow the command only until you give another to follow. (After all, you want the game to be fun, not impossible!)

Begin the game and allow students to play for three minutes or so; then call out the instruction that one team's members can't use their left arms. Allow a few more minutes; then call out that the other team's members can't use their hands. Continue regularly calling out different instructions that will prohibit players from using one body part or another, such as arms, legs, feet, and so on.

After students have played for several minutes, stop the game and discuss:

How did the special instructions affect your ability to play this game?

How was this game like losing important things or people in real life? It's hard to function when you are missing something.

How does that kind of loss affect our ability to cope with life? It makes life a lot harder.

Abandonment

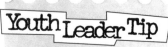

Junior highers have different levels of physical coordination. When possible, try to equalize the playing field by substituting balloons where balls might typically be used for a game, having students sit rather than stand, or having each student place one hand behind his or her back. This way, those who aren't as talented in sports have a fighting chance to do just as well as your athletic superstars.

Explain: **Although other things and people are important and make life more meaningful, we can't count on them. We can lose everything in a heartbeat. But as we'll see today, only God will never abandon us.**

This step shows that God will never abandon us.

You'll need Several Bibles, copies of "Job's Story" (p. 60) and pens or pencils.

Divide students into groups of four or five; then distribute Bibles, "Job's Story" and pens or pencils. Assign each group one of the following Scripture passages: Job 1; Job 2; Job 38; 42:1-6 . Instruct groups to read their assigned passages and answer the questions on their handouts that pertain only to their assigned passage.

Allow several minutes for groups to work; then mix up the groups, forming new groups of three. (Each group should contain students from previous groups.) Instruct students to share their previous groups' answers and complete the remaining sections of their handouts.

When everyone has finished, discuss:

What's your reaction to what Job experienced?

What's your reaction to the way Job handled his experience?

How would you handle something like that?

What did God teach Job through this experience? That He was always there with Job and that He had a plan for Job.

What can we learn about God from Job's experience?

Explain: **God's plans are so much bigger and greater than what we can see. Even when we feel like we've lost everything, God hasn't abandoned us. And He never will.**

Read Job 42:10-17; then discuss: **Why do you think God blessed Job with so much in the end? If He hadn't, would that have meant God had abandoned him?**

Conclude: **The biggest blessing is a growing relationship with God, which far surpasses even the coolest stuff and closest friends or family.**

You'll need Several Bibles, a white board and a dry-erase marker.

Distribute Bibles; then have students take turns reading Job 1—2 a few verses at a time. After the passage has been read, explain that students are going to pretend that Job is filing an insurance claim for everything he lost. Ask students to name the things Job lost and use their responses to create a list on the white board.

As a group, read Job 38 and 42:1-6; then ask students to help you create a second list, showing what Job *gained* through this experience. These answers are less tangible. If students need help with this, here are some suggested answers: a new knowledge of God, insight into who his real friends were, a new sense of priorities and an appreciation for what God had given him.

When you've compiled the second list discuss:

Why did Job lose so much? Because Satan wanted to destroy him.

How do you feel about God letting this happen to Job?

Why do you think God let this happen?

How would you feel if you were in Job's situation?

How did Job seem to feel? He was grieved and hurt, but he still trusted God.

Where was God when Job was suffering? He was right there.

How did God respond to Job's calls to Him? God reminded Job of His power, position, presence and plan.

How do you think Job felt when he discovered God hadn't abandoned him?

How did this experience change Job? He learned more about God—and so did his "friends"!

Read Job 42:10-17 and discuss:

Why do you think God gave Job twice as much? To bless him for his faithfulness.

How do you think Job felt?

What if God had given him nothing back?

What had Job already gained? The key point to make here is that Job had already gained a new appreciation of God (see Bible Bonus Note).

Option 3  Pulse Points

You'll need Your Bible, an orange, a white board, a dry-erase marker and transparent tape.

The Big Idea

God will never abandon us.

The Big Question

What does it mean that God will never abandon us?

1. God is there, even when we feel like we've lost everything.

Read Job 1—2. While you're reading the Scripture, peel an orange as students watch. Pull off one section of orange peel every time the Bible describes something Job lost. Continue until you've read through the passage and peeled the entire orange; then point out: **Job experienced incredible loss. But throughout life, we all experience loss to some degree. External things are stripped away: family, friends, money, belongings, health, prestige, reputation. Our lives change; we feel exposed and vulnerable. But God is still with us. God holds us together as the orange is still held together in spite of losing its peeling.**

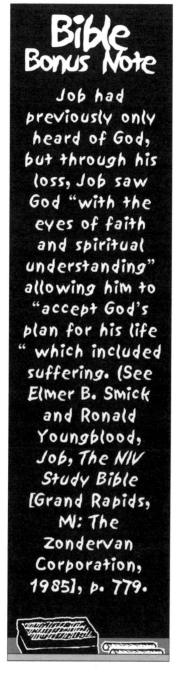

Bible Bonus Note

Job had previously only heard of God, but through his loss, Job saw God "with the eyes of faith and spiritual understanding" allowing him to "accept God's plan for his life " which included suffering. (See Elmer B. Smick and Ronald Youngblood, *Job, The NIV Study Bible* [Grand Rapids, MI: The Zondervan Corporation, 1985], p. 779.

2. God is there, even when we don't see Him.

Read Job 38 and explain that God was present in Job's life in many powerful ways that Job couldn't see or took for granted. Ask: **What are some similar indications of God's constant presence in our lives?** Write students' responses on the white board.

Read Job 42:1-6. Point out that because of his incredible loss, Job experienced God in deeper, more significant ways than he had before. When we lose people and things that are important to us, we can experience God differently in those times—and we can realize that He's still there, even when we feel like we've lost everything.

3. God is there in good times and bad.

Read Job 42:10-17. As you're reading, tape the peeling back onto the orange, restoring it as much as possible. Explain: **Eventually, Job got back twice as much from God. But God's presence wasn't in those things. Job knew God was with him because he had seen God's presence in the darkest times. In the good times, enjoy God's blessings without trusting in them as indicators of God's presence or what holds our lives together.** Hold up the orange and discuss: **Considering what this orange has been through, what would a smart orange be trusting to keep it together at this point?**

Conclude: **Just as the orange shouldn't trust the peeling to keep it together, we shouldn't trust the temporary people and things in our lives. We should put our trust in God, who's always there—in good times and bad.**

NOTES

STEP 3 MOVING ON

This step examines where we're putting our trust.

Option 1 Chat Room

You'll need Paper and pens or pencils.

Distribute paper and pens or pencils and instruct students to list 10 people or things that are important to them. Allow a few minutes; then divide students into pairs and instruct partners to discuss how they would react if they lost each of those items on their lists.

Allow several minutes for students to share; then discuss:

Considering how temporary these things and people are, where should we be placing our trust? On God.

If we build our lives on these things, what will happen to us when they're taken away? We won't have them anymore; we will have difficulty adjusting.

If we build our lives on Christ, how will we react when those things are taken away? We will always have Jesus Christ to depend on. He will provide what we need.

How do we know what we're building our lives on? We can look at what is most important to us—those things we can't or won't let go of. What do we spend our money and time on?

How can we build our lives on Christ? By spending time getting to know Him, through prayer, Bible study, worship, spending time with other Christians.

How do we appreciate the things and people in our lives without trusting in them? We can enjoy and appreciate them while we have them with us. We can spend time and build good memories with people we love. We can take care of the things we own but not become overly attached to them.

What does it mean to trust Christ instead of the things and people around us? To put Him first in your life.

Where are you placing your trust? Give students a moment or two of silence to reflect on this question before moving on to the next step.

Option 2  Real Life

You'll need Just yer pearly whites (you need them for smilin')!

Share the following story:

Joe was a pretty lucky guy. His parents had good jobs, and they lived in a nice house. He had everything he needed and most of what he wanted. He was pretty popular, and he had lots of friends he had grown up with. His family got along pretty well. They went to church, and he was involved in the youth group.

One day, Joe's luck ran out. He got home from school one day to a nearly empty house. As soon as he walked in, he could see something was wrong. His family's belongings were scattered everywhere, and a lot of it was missing. Someone had broken into their house and taken everything of value. Their TVs and stereos were gone. His mother's jewelry box was empty. They had even taken his Play Station and his CD collection.

As Joe was walking through the house, trying to figure out what all was missing, there was a knock on the door. He answered it to see two police officers standing there. They told Joe they were sorry, but his family had been in a car accident—hit by a drunk driver. Their car had gone over the side of a bridge and everyone had died. The police wanted him to come with them to identify the bodies and try to contact someone who could take care of him.

As Joe walked out to the police car in a daze, someone from his church drove up. "Joe!" she called. "I came to tell your family what happened. We called a special meeting at the church, and everyone was there except your family. The building suddenly collapsed, and everyone except me was killed because I went outside to get something out of my car. The building is completely destroyed!"

As she was still speaking, another family friend drove up. "Joe," he said, "I hate to tell you this, but your grandma has passed away, along with all your aunts, uncles and cousins. They were having a get-together at your grandma's house when a tornado came through and wiped away everything. I was the only one to survive."

Suddenly Joe heard a huge explosion behind him, then someone yelled "Fire!" He turned around to see his house burning to the ground. "Must have been a gas leak," said one of the police officers.

Joe couldn't believe what was happening. He felt dizzy and fell to the ground with his head in his hands. He had lost everything! He had no money, no belongings, no family, no one to look after him. What was he going to do now?

Discuss:

What did Joe lose? Nearly everything.

How would you react if you were Joe?

How do you think Joe will react?

What are Joe's options?

How might this story turn out if Joe has been trusting in the people and things around him? He might become angry and bitter, or withdraw, or completely give up.

How might this story turn out if Joe has been trusting in God and His constant presence? He would have some tough times ahead, but he could turn to God to help him through the difficulties.

How can Joe be reminded that God will never abandon him? Through the comfort and prayers of others, through Scripture he might have memorized, by relying on what he knows about God.

What might he learn about God from this experience? His faith would grow strong as he sees God's comfort and provision.

NOTES

Option 3 — Tough Questions

You'll need Just the questions below.

1. **How can we be sure God will never abandon us?** Being sure is a matter of trust. Because we know God and His character, we can choose to believe His promises in the Bible. God has promised to never abandon us, and He has been faithful to that promise for generations.

2. **If God is always with me, why do I sometimes feel like He's so far away?** Our feelings aren't always good indicators of God's presence. Our feelings are affected by a variety of factors, and we can't trust them to tell us about God's presence or feelings toward us. Usually, if we feel like God is far away, it's because we're feeling bad about ourselves, or we've allowed a barrier of sin to block our relationship with God.

3. **So what should we do about the important people and things in our lives?** We should be grateful for the blessings God gives us and for the benefits we enjoy in life. But we should always remember that they're temporary, and only God will never abandon us. That doesn't mean we have to get rid of everything or refuse to have close relationships. We just have to remember that they don't last.

4. **Is it wrong to feel bad when we lose something or someone important to us?** It's OK to grieve when we experience loss. We should always acknowledge when we're hurting. Grief should inspire us to turn to God for comfort and thus help us grow closer to Him.

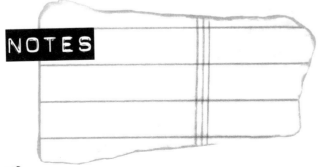

NOTES

STEP 4 — MOVING OUT

This step challenges students to put their faith in God this week.

Option 1 — Light the Fire

You'll need Poster board and colored felt-tip pens.

Ask students to name things that people tend to put their trust in. As they call them out, write them on the poster paper with different colored pens. When finished, point out how flimsy the poster is and explain: **Just like this poster can rip and tear and fade, so can the things we tend to rely on.**

Tell students you'd like to give them an opportunity to make a commitment to trust God instead of the things they listed. If students are ready to make that commitment, they should tear off a section of the poster and throw it away as a symbol to trust God instead.

Point out to students that we can't see God's presence, but He's always there. Then close in prayer, thanking God for being worthy of our trust.

> **Note:** For more detailed information on leading students to Christ, see the student article from **Pulse #1:** *Christianity, the Basics*, pages 95-96.

Option 2 — Fired Up

You'll need Lyrics to worship songs that talk about trusting only in God (and some type of accompaniment if desired).

Explain to students they are going to have an opportunity to respond to God's constant presence by worshiping Him in song. Spend some time singing worship songs that talk about trusting only in God.

Between songs, invite students to confess silently or aloud their tendencies to trust in other people or things besides God.

Close in a prayer of confession and commitment to trust in God alone.

Option 3  Spread the Fire

You'll need A blow dryer, a paper heart, a book, a football (or soccer ball or basketball) and a picture of a group of people.

Explain: **The people you know at school who don't know Jesus are probably relying on other things for comfort and strength. The problem is that any of these can be taken away. Then what are they left with?**

Hold up the items one at a time, asking students to say a silent sentence prayer for one or two people they know who are relying on one of these things rather than Jesus. As you hold up each item one at a time, explain that the blow dryer represents physical appearance, the heart represents romance, the book represents grades, the ball represents athletic ability, and the picture of people represents friends.

Close in prayer, asking God to give us all courage to share about Him with those who are likely to be let down by these temporary items.

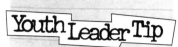

Youth Leader Tip

At the end of this session, you may want to invite students to talk with you about what it means to put their trust in Christ. Make yourself available to answer questions afterward. Be sure you place yourself in a location where students won't feel conspicuous or self-conscious if they want to talk with you.

NOTES

Job's Story

Group 1

Read Job 1 and answer these questions:

What did Job experience in this passage?

How did Job react to what he experienced?

Group 2

Read Job 2 and answer these questions:

What did Job experience in this passage?

How did Job react to what he experienced?

Group 3

Read Job 38 and 42:1-6 and answer these questions:

What did Job experience in this passage?

How did Job react to what he experienced?

Devotions in Motion

WEEK FOUR: ABANDONMENT

DAY 1

FAST FACTS
Micah 7:7 is calling your name.

God Says
Eric's mom has been diagnosed with cancer. For the first few weeks, Eric prayed all the time. He was frustrated because he thought that the more he prayed, the quicker she would get better. When a month went by and his mom still had cancer, he stopped praying because he thought it wasn't doing any good.

I Do
Have you ever felt like Eric? Have you prayed for something painful to go away and it didn't?

How does this verse in Micah make you feel about prayer?

Here's a bigger question: How does that make you feel about God?

Next time you're disappointed with the way God seems to answer your prayer in a different way than you expected, remember one thing: God is good. He can't help but be good. How would knowing this change your feelings about prayer? How would it make you more patient and help you wait for His answer?

FOLD HERE --

DAY 4

QUICK QUESTIONS
Hey, do you know where the book of Psalms is? Well then, check out Psalm 121:1,2!

God Says
What are three ways you can help your mom or dad when they get home tired from a long day at work?

1. _____
2. _____
3. _____

I Do
Write down Psalm 121:1,2 and put it in a place where you stand frequently (like your school locker or your bathroom mirror). Whenever you see the verse, remember that God is ready to help you—anytime, anywhere.

What are two ways that knowing that God is your help would make you feel differently about your day?

QUICK QUESTIONS

Like water and fire? Read Isaiah 43:1,2.

God Says

Which would be the greater loss?

☐ Your home   or   ☐ your homework

☐ A game   or   ☐ a sock

☐ Your lunch   or   ☐ your bike

☐ Your money   or   ☐ your video games

I Do

There's not a single person alive who hasn't lost something. Sometimes we lose really important things, like people, parents, siblings, friends, other students at school, teachers, neighbors—none of them are going to be with us forever.

BUT wait, there is someone we're not going to lose. Or maybe more properly, someone who will never lose us!

What is the promise God makes in Isaiah? Do you believe that? He doesn't lose sight of us.

Spend two minutes right now thanking God that He doesn't lose sight of us.

FOLD HERE

FAST FACTS

Nahum 1:7 is sweet reading.

God Says

Fred has a routine for when his parents fight. He goes to his room, turns up the radio to drown out his parents' voices and waits about 90 minutes before he goes back out. Fred hates it when his parents fight.

He learned at youth group that we can go to God when we are in trouble. Fred knows that, but he doesn't know how to do it when his parents are yelling at each other downstairs.

I Do

What would you tell Fred?

What does it mean to have God as our refuge in times of trouble?

Now pray for God to remind you to go to Him the next time life gets hard, which might be at this very moment.

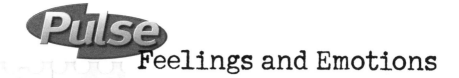
SESSIONFIVESESSIONFIVESESSIONFIVE

The Big Idea

God wants us to give up on violence and call on Him.

Session Aims

In this session you will guide students to:

- Understand how God feels about violence;
- Recognize the presence of violence in their own lives;
- Respond by turning away from violence and turning toward God.

The Biggest Verse

"Let everyone call urgently on God. Let them give up their evil ways and their violence." Jonah 3:8

Other Important Verses

Jonah 1—3; Matthew 12:33-35; Philippians 4:8

Violence

STEP
MOVING IN

This step helps students realize the destructive nature of violence.

Option 1 — Move It

You'll need Two student volunteers.

Ahead of time, have the two volunteers prepare a staged fight at the start of your meeting. They shouldn't actually hit each other, but they should act pretty angry—as if they want to hit each other. Help them come up with something realistic to be angry about (both liking the same person, losing a favorite article of clothing, breaking a new CD player, etc.). **Option:** If you're not comfortable asking students to do this, try adult volunteers or parents.

As you greet students, the confrontation should begin. Don't let on that it's been prepared and practiced. Just before the two volunteers get to the point where they might actually hit each other, stop them and have them take a seat. Explain: **I've got to let you in on something. I actually asked these two to pretend that they were really angry at each other. Why? Because today we're talking about something that you see almost every day, and often in situations similar to what just happened. That something is violence.**

Stand up if any of the following statements describe how you felt during the conflict you just observed. (If you want to get students really moving, have them move to a certain wall if they felt what you're describing below.)

Read the following responses one at a time, giving students a chance to stand (or move to the wall):

You wanted to see what would happen if they actually hit each other.

You hoped they'd hit each other.

You hoped they'd stop fighting.

You felt uncomfortable watching.

You wanted an adult to intervene.

You didn't want an adult to intervene.

Ask students to sit down; then discuss:

What surprises you about how you felt when you were watching the fight?

How is this like how you feel at school when you see similar things happening?

How is this unlike how you feel at school when you see similar things happening?

Conclude: **Well, today we're going to take a closer look at violence and explore it with honesty and a commitment to understanding what Scripture has to say about it.**

Option 2 — Chat Room

You'll need A TV, a VCR and a blank videotape.

Ahead of time, videotape several clips from TV shows and/or movies that show various types of violence. Be sure the scenes are violent enough to be obvious but not enough to horrify or upset students or their parents.

Greet students and show the videotape you created; then discuss:

Why is violence so easy to find on TV and in movies? How about in our society?

Why is it so easy to give in to violence?

What were the results of the violence in these clips?

What are the results of violence in real life? Suffering, injury, death, more violence, etc.

How realistic is the violence we see on TV or movies? How realistic are its results? Usually not very realistic.

When have you been affected by violence?

What do you consider to be violent? What isn't violent?

How should we react to threats of violence?

How should we react when we see violence?

Summarize: **As we'll see today, violence is always destructive, no matter what form it takes.**

NOTES

Option 3  Fun and Games

You'll need Paper plates, rubber bands and a stopwatch (or a watch with a seconds indicator).

Greet students and divide them into pairs. Explain that they will be doing a little target practice today. Here's how it works: **Give each pair several paper plates and several rubber bands. Partners must remain five steps apart from each other at all times. One partner will toss the paper plates in the air while the other will shoot the rubber bands at the paper plates. After one minute, partners should switch roles. The pairs will have two minutes to shoot their paper plates as many times as they can.** Congratulate the team who hit their plates the most often.

After the game, discuss:

How was this game like violence in real life? We were shooting at something.

How was it different? We didn't hurt anyone (hopefully!).

In real life, what are the results of violence? Suffering, injury, death, more violence, etc.

Does violence ever have truly positive results? No. **Why not?** Because it is the result of anger and bitterness, and it causes pain and suffering.

Sum up: **As we'll see today, violence is always destructive, no matter what form it takes.**

STEP MOVING UP

This step helps students understand how much God hates violence.

Option 1  Move It

You'll need Several Bibles, paper and pens or pencils.

Divide students into at least three groups of five or six and distribute Bibles, paper and pens or pencils to each group. Set up this activity by telling students that a church across town has had trouble coming up with enough Sunday School teachers, so they've asked your group to teach three of their Sunday School classes—on Jonah 3:1-10.

Share the following background from Jonah 1—2: **When God asked Jonah to go and preach to the city of Nineveh and warn them of their wickedness, Jonah instead ran away. He got on a ship headed for Tarshish, a city in the opposite direction of Nineveh. However, a big storm came and threatened the ship, at which point the sailors cast lots to find out who was responsible for their calamity. The lot fell to Jonah, so the sailors threw him overboard in an effort to**

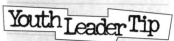

Youth Leader Tip

When you create the videotape of violent clips, be sure to draw from a variety of sources. Some programs to consider include children's cartoons, action movies, police dramas, teen horror films and even daytime talk shows.

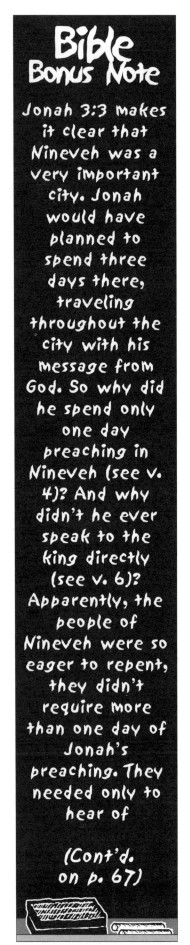

Bible Bonus Note

Jonah 3:3 makes it clear that Nineveh was a very important city. Jonah would have planned to spend three days there, traveling throughout the city with his message from God. So why did he spend only one day preaching in Nineveh (see v. 4)? And why didn't he ever speak to the king directly (see v. 6)? Apparently, the people of Nineveh were so eager to repent, they didn't require more than one day of Jonah's preaching. They needed only to hear of

(Cont'd. on p. 67)

save their ship. **The Lord provided a huge fish to swallow Jonah. He was inside the fish for three days and three nights. While inside, Jonah realized his need to obey God—the one who had saved his life.** Have students follow along as you read through Jonah 3.

Assign one group to teach the children, another group to teach the youth and the third group to teach the adults. Instruct each group to come up with a two-minute skit that depicts what Jonah would do and say to people in their assigned age group today.

Give groups five minutes to prepare their skits. Have groups present their dramas, beginning with the group assigned to teach the children, then youth and then adults.

When groups are finished, discuss:

What did you learn about this passage from what you taught?

What did you learn about this passage from being taught?

What's the meaning of this story?

How did God feel about the violence and other behavior of the Ninevites? He was angry enough that He wanted to destroy them unless they repented.

What was God's plan? To send Jonah to preach to them and give them an opportunity to repent.

Why do you think God hates violence? Because it causes suffering and death, often to innocent people.

Summarize: **God hates violence because it hurts people and pushes God out of our lives.**

Option 2  Chat Room

You'll need Several Bibles, copies of "Correct the Mistakes" (p. 71) and pens or pencils.

Divide students into pairs and distribute a Bible, "Correct the Mistakes" and a pen or pencil to each pair. Share the following background from Jonah 1—2: **When God asked Jonah to go and preach to the city of Nineveh and warn them of their wickedness, Jonah instead ran away. He got on a ship headed for Tarshish, a city in the opposite direction of Nineveh. However, a big storm came and threatened the ship, at which point the sailors cast lots to find out who was responsible for their calamity. The lot fell to Jonah, so the sailors threw him overboard in an effort to save their ship. The Lord provided a huge fish to swallow Jonah. He was inside the fish for three days and three nights. While inside, Jonah realized his need to obey God—the one who had saved his life.**

Using the handout, have students correct the mistakes in the bogus retelling of Jonah 3, so that it matches the Bible account. One person should read the passage while the other person follows along, making the corrections.

When students have finished, go through the handout together, letting them call out the mistakes they found and the correct answers. You can refer below for the correct information. The corrections are in parentheses.

Discuss:

Why did God send Jonah to speak to the Ninevites? To warn them of their impending destruction, giving them a chance to repent before it was too late.

How did God feel about the violence and other behavior of the Ninevites? He was angry enough that He wanted to destroy them unless they repented.

How did God feel about the Ninevites themselves? He obviously loved them because He sent Jonah to warn them.

What was God's plan to deal with the Ninevites? He would destroy them if they didn't repent.

Why did God change His plans? Because they repented.

How do you think the Ninevites felt after God changed His plans?

How do you think God feels about violence in our world? The same way.

Why does God hate violence? Because it causes suffering and death, often to innocent people.

How do you think God wants us to respond to violence? By working to avoid or prevent it from happening.

Explain: **God hates violence because it hurts people and pushes God out of our lives.**

Corrections for "Correct the Mistakes": Then the word of the Lord came to Jonah a second time: "Go to the *small* (great) city of Nineveh and proclaim to it the *song* (message) I give you."

Jonah obeyed the word of the Lord and went to Nineveh. Now Nineveh was a very *confusing* (important) city—a visit required three *aspirin* (days). On the first day, Jonah started into the *song* (city). He *sang* (proclaimed): "Forty more days and Nineveh will be *unrecognizable* (overturned)." The Ninevites believed God. They declared a *holiday* (fast), and all of them, from the *oldest* (greatest) to the *youngest* (least), put on *robes* (sackcloth).

When the news reached the king of Nineveh, he rose from his *chair* (throne), took off his *T-shirt* (royal robes), covered himself with *burlap* (sackcloth) and sat down in the *sun* (dust).

Then he issued a proclamation in Nineveh: "By the decree of the king and his *pets* (nobles): Do not let any man or *plant* (beast), herd or flock, taste anything; do not let them eat or drink. But let man and beast be covered with *mosquito netting* (sackcloth). Let everyone call urgently on God. Let them give up their *selfish* (evil) ways and their violence. Who knows? God may yet relent and with compassion turn from His fierce anger so that we will not *suffer* (perish)."

When God saw what they did and how they turned from their evil ways, He had compassion and did not bring upon them the *inconvenience* (destruction) He had threatened.

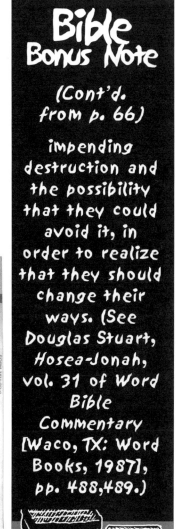

Bible Bonus Note

(Cont'd. from p. 66)

impending destruction and the possibility that they could avoid it, in order to realize that they should change their ways. (See Douglas Stuart, *Hosea-Jonah*, vol. 31 of *Word Bible Commentary* [Waco, TX: Word Books, 1987], pp. 488,489.)

Option 3  Pulse Points

You'll need Your Bible, a piece of fruit that's easy to smash (and messy—such as a peach, a melon or a banana), two plastic tablecloths, a hammer (or large, heavy item you can smash something with), a white board and a dry-erase marker.

Ahead of time, put a plastic tablecloth on the table and the floor where you'll be smashing the fruit.

The Big Idea

God hates violence.

The Big Question

Why does God hate violence?

1. Violence hurts people.

Smash the piece of fruit. Make sure it makes as big a mess as possible, getting it on you and some of the students. Explain: **Violence hurts people. And like this fruit, it doesn't affect just its victim. It hurts the person doing the violence as well as other people.**

Read Jonah 3:1-4. Continue: **God hated the wickedness He saw in Nineveh. But He also loved the people, so He sent Jonah to warn them to turn away from violence. God sent Jonah to warn them of the coming judgment upon their city.**

2. Violence pushes God out of our lives.

Explain: **When we rely on violence, we are refusing to depend on God and do things His way.** Ask students to name characteristics of God's way of doing things (just, fair, merciful, forgiving, etc). As they share, write their responses on the white board. Then have students name characteristics of violent behavior (selfish, impatience, unjust, etc.) and write those responses next to the first list.

Read Jonah 3:5-10 and conclude: **God changed His plan when the people turned away from their violence and invited God into their lives. As a result, He forgave them and Nineveh was not destroyed.**

NOTES

STEP 3 — MOVING ON

This step reveals to students all the ways that violence occurs around them and in their own lives.

Option 1  Chat Room

You'll need A large piece of newsprint, a felt-tip pen and masking tape.

Draw an outline of a human body on the newsprint and tape it up where everyone can see it. Have students look at the various parts of the body and call out ways the parts of the body can be used for violence. For example, hands can be used to hit, eyes can be used to glare, the mind can be used for thoughts of hatred and the behind can be used for sitting in a movie theater to watch a violent movie. As students call out ideas, label the various parts of the body with ways they can be used for violence. Discuss:

What's your reaction to seeing all the ways violence can be present in our lives?

Were you surprised? Were you reminded of hidden violence in your life?

Why do you think it's so easy to overlook violence in our lives? Because we see it represented everywhere in the media until we are numb.

When we evaluate our lives, who should we compare ourselves to? Jesus.

Why is it important to be aware of the many forms violence can take in our lives? We can't avoid it if we aren't aware of it.

How does God feel about the violence in our lives? He hates it.

How can we become more aware of the violence in our lives? By asking God to make us aware of it by realizing the many forms violence can take.

How should we respond to the violence we find in our lives? By working to avoid or prevent it from happening.

Option 2  Real Life

You'll need Guts. You're a junior high youth leader, aren't you?

Share the following case study:

> When I was in sixth grade, I wasn't afraid to go to school. But then in seventh grade I heard about all these shootings all over the country. Kids my age, some even younger, bringing guns to school and killing other kids. Now my school doesn't just have fire drills, we have bomb drills and kids-with-guns drills. I heard that next month we're getting a metal detector at the school entrance.
>
> My older brother in college didn't have to go through all this. When he was my age, it was rare for a kid to bring a knife to school. Now I know tons of kids who bring not just knives but guns. I can think of five kids right now who bring guns to school, sometimes keeping them in their lockers.
>
> I don't want to go to school. It's too scary.

Discuss:

How are your feelings similar to this student's?

How are they different?

Do you think junior high schools are scarier and more violent now than they were 10 or 20 years ago?

What is your school doing to respond to school violence?

How does God want us to respond to school violence? By working to avoid it or prevent it from happening.

If you know someone who brings a gun to school, should you tell a teacher, or should you keep silent?

Option 3  Tough Questions

You'll need Nothing but the questions below.

1. **If God hates violence, how can we defend ourselves if we're attacked?** Sometimes the best thing to do is to just walk away from violence. But if you absolutely have to fight back, it's OK to defend yourself from harm. Just don't get carried away by the desire to hurt someone else.

2. **How can we avoid violence, since it seems to be everywhere?** We probably can't always avoid violence, but we can refuse to participate in it. And we can encourage others to turn away from violence.

3. **If God hates violence, why is the Bible so violent?** The Bible reflects real life and the way God relates to people in the real world. It doesn't provide a picture of a perfect world, but a world that is contaminated by sin.

4. **What are we supposed to do when we see violence?** If it's safe for us to stop the violence, we should stop it. If not, we should get help from someone who can, such as an adult, a school administrator, a police officer or a security guard.

5. **Are violent thoughts just as bad as violent actions? What about watching violent movies or saying violent words?** Any type of violence is equally wrong in God's eyes. Watching movies or saying violent words makes those thoughts start to take root in your mind and can affect you later. It's best to avoid them and stay as focused on God as possible (see Matthew 12:33-35; Philippians 4:8).

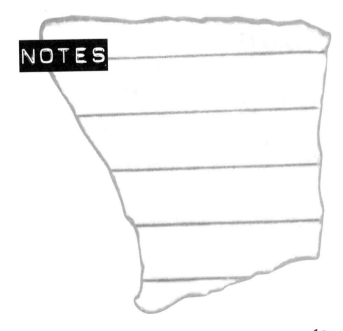

STEP 4 — MOVING OUT

This step provides an opportunity for students to reject violence and turn to God today.

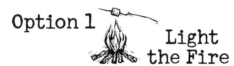

Option 1 — Light the Fire

You'll need Copies of "Last Month" (p. 72) and pens or pencils.

Explain: **I want you to think about all the kinds of violence you've seen in the last month.** Distribute "Last Month" and pens or pencils; then continue: **Circle any of the following that you've seen or done and make sure to add your own if you can think of other violent things you've seen or done.**

Give students a few minutes to do this, and then ask them to think about what they'd like to see in the next month. Ask them to cross out anything they'd like to avoid seeing or participating in during the next month. Form small groups of three or four and instruct them to pray for one another, asking God to help them reject the kinds of violent things they've seen, said and done in the past.

Option 2 — Fired Up

You'll need Copies of "When I Get Angry" (p. 73) and pens or pencils.

Explain: **There's a strong connection between violence and anger, so I want us to finish this lesson by thinking about what we tend to do when we get angry.** Distribute "When I Get Angry" and pens or pencils as you continue: **Take a few minutes to write down what you tend to do when you get angry at the people listed.**

Explain: **Now I'd like you to write down what you think God wants you to do when you get angry at these people.** After a minute or two, instruct students to write down one thing they could do this week that would help them act like God wants them to when they get angry.

After their lists are complete, continue: **Now I'd like you to circle one or two things on this list of things you could do this week that you can actually see yourself doing. Sure, it might be hard to do, but you know you can do it.**

If you have time, ask students to form small groups of three to pray for one another, asking God to give them strength to act like He wants them to.

Option 3 — Spread the Fire

You'll need A bedsheet or large piece of cloth, colored felt-tip pens or fabric paints, a plastic tarp and masking tape or tacks.

Explain: **Violence affects your witness for Christ. Violent thoughts and behavior get in the way of showing other people the difference Jesus can make in a person's life. You can share the gospel by the way you live.**

Encourage students to think of at least one type of violence that is present in their lives. Then have them consider all the specific people, especially non-Christians, who would be impacted if they chose to turn away from that violence and turn to God instead.

While students are thinking, spread out the plastic tarp and lay the bedsheet or large piece of cloth and felt-tip pens or fabric paints on top of the tarp (in case the pens or paints soak through the cloth).

Instruct students to fill the cloth with all the names of the people they've thought of who would be impacted in some way if they chose to turn away from violence in their lives. When they're finished, hang the banner in your room as a reminder of the powerful influence of turning away from violence.

Challenge students to actively turn away from violence during the next month; then challenge them to go one step further and share their faith with one of the people they listed on the banner. They may find that their behavior has made a difference in the other person's openness to the gospel.

Close with a prayer of commitment, encouraging each person to say aloud the name of one person to impact for Christ by turning away from violence.

NOTES

Correct the Mistakes

Find and correct the mistakes in this retelling of Jonah 3:1-10.

Then the word of the Lord came to Jonah a second time: "Go to the small city of Nineveh and proclaim to it the song I give you."

Jonah obeyed the word of the Lord and went to Nineveh. Now Nineveh was a very confusing city—a visit required three aspirins. On the first day, Jonah started into the song. He sang: "Forty more days and Nineveh will be unrecognizable." The Ninevites believed God. They declared a holiday, and all of them, from the oldest to the youngest, put on robes.

When the news reached the king of Nineveh, he rose from his chair, took off his T-shirt, covered himself with burlap and sat down in the sun.

Then he issued a proclamation in Nineveh: "By the decree of the king and his pets: Do not let any man or plant, herd or flock, taste anything; do not let them eat or drink. But let man and beast be covered with mosquito netting. Let everyone call urgently on God. Let them give up their selfish ways and their violence. Who knows? God may yet relent and with compassion turn from His fierce anger so that we will not suffer."

When God saw what they did and how they turned from their evil ways, He had compassion and did not bring upon them the inconvenience He had threatened.

Last Month

Put a check in the box next to any of the following that you've said or done:

❏ Yelled at a brother or sister

❏ Hit or pushed a brother or sister

❏ Played video games or computer games that were violent

❏ Played a game in which people pretended to shoot or kill each other

❏ Saw a fight at school between two guys

❏ Saw a fight at school between two girls

❏ Held a gun

❏ Held a knife

❏ Brought a gun to school

❏ Brought a knife to school

❏ Gave someone a dirty look at school

❏ Watched a movie in which someone was shot or stabbed or punched

❏ Saw a TV show in which someone was shot or stabbed or punched

❏ Listened to music that talked about hurting other people

❏ Listened to music that talked about hurting yourself

72

When I Get Angry

WHEN I'M angry at	What I do NOW	What God wants ME to do	ONE thing I could do this WEEK
MY PARENTS			
MYSELF			
MY SIBLINGS			
MY FRIENDS			
PEOPLE I don't like			

Devotions in Motion

WEEK FIVE: VIOLENCE

DAY 1

QUICK QUESTIONS

Do you know someone who Talks a loT? Read James 1:19,20.

God Says

According To James, label These situations as slow (S) or quick (Q).

_____ Your friend is gossiping abouT you aT school.

_____ Your mom is explaining how she wanTs you To clean The baThroom.

_____ You sTub your Toe.

_____ You sTrike ouT in The championship game.

I Do

IT's hard To be slow To anger, isn'T iT? WhaT are The benefiTs of being quick To anger?

How abouT The benefiTs of being slow To anger?

When do you Tend To be quick To become angry?

How could you acT differenTly The nexT Time ThaT Thing happens?

FOLD HERE

DAY 4

FAST FACTS

How long will iT Take for you To geT To Luke 6:27-31?

God Says

You are on your way home from your friend's house and you are approached by a bully who wanTs To fighT wiTh you. WhaT are Two ways you could respond? WriTe a godly choice and a worldly choice and whaT The resulT(s) of each would be.

Godly Choice   Worldly Choice

I Do

Everyone is TempTed To reTaliaTe when someone has been violenT wiTh Them. BuT Jesus' words in Luke 6 Tell us noT To fighT back or Try To geT even.

WriTe down on The boTTom of This page whaT you are going To do The nexT Time someone eggs you on and you feel like fighTing back. Here's an example: I promise To be more like God and Turn away from violence The nexT Time iT comes my way!

FAST FACTS

Read about fools in Ecclesiastes 7:9.

God Says

Mike was a bully. When he got angry at school he would push people around and try to take their lunch money. People were scared of him for a while. Pretty soon though, people just thought he was foolish and were no longer afraid of him.

Mike went with his younger brother to youth group and realized that he wanted to change his ways. But no one there would take him seriously. Mike felt kinda dumb for the way he had been acting, but he didn't know what else to do.

I Do.

Have you ever gotten angry and then felt foolish afterwards? It is not a good feeling. So many times when we are angry, we act like fools. We don't think clearly, we lash out at others and sometimes we even become violent.

The next time you're feeling angry, stop and ask God to help you know what to do. And don't be surprised if He wants you to talk to whoever is making you angry and forgive them.

FOLD HERE

QUICK QUESTIONS

For great verses that you might not have read before, turn to Matthew 5:23,24!

God Says

Candace and Guadalupe got in a big fight. Candace's parents gave her two tickets to a concert for her birthday. She could ask anyone to go with her. She did not ask Guadalupe to go because she thought she would not like the music. Guadalupe was hurt and became very angry at Candace. They soon stopped talking and spread rumors about one another. One day Candace confronted Guadalupe and explained the situation. The more they talked, the more they realized that they had nothing to be mad about.

I Do.

When we don't make things right, our feelings fester up like a cut we don't take care of and infect us with anger and bitterness.

Write down the names of two people who you need to get right with.

Now pray that God would give you courage to live out Matthew 5:23,24 rather than give in to the temptation of becoming angry and bitter.

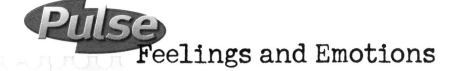

Feelings and Emotions

SESSIONSIXSESSIONSIXSESSIONSIXSESSIONSIX

The Big Idea

Suicide may seem like the way out when you're struggling, but Jesus is the only real answer.

Session Aims

In this session you will guide students to:

- Understand that everyone faces desperate times;
- Experience the hope Jesus offers in the midst of tough times;
- Celebrate life in Jesus in at least one tangible way.

Suicide

The Biggest Verse

"So Judas threw the money into the temple and left. Then he went away and hanged himself."
Matthew 27:5

Other Important Verses

Exodus 20:13; Matthew 27:1-10; Luke 23:39-43; Ephesians 2:8,9

STEP

MOVING IN

This step establishes that we all face desperate times.

Option 1 Move It

You'll need To show up with this book!

Greet students and survey the group: **What would you do if . . .**

- One day you woke up and realized you had shrunk to only an inch tall?
- Some moldy food in the fridge mutated and attacked you in your sleep?
- You turned on the TV and every station was broadcasting different parts of your life—someone had been videotaping you all along?
- A group of aliens landed on your lawn and demanded that you go back with them to serve as their cook?

Explain: **These situations were just for fun, but in real life we all face desperate times when we feel like there's no way out. In those times, suicide may seem like a way out. But suicide never solves anything, and it's never the answer. As we'll see, Jesus is the only real answer to our problems.**

Option 2 Chat Room

You'll need An overhead projector and a transparency copy of "Startling Statistics" (p. 85).

Greet students and explain that today you'll be talking about a very serious topic; then use the overhead projector to share the suicide statistics. After pointing out each one, discuss:

What's your reaction to these statistics?

Why do you think suicide is so prevalent in our society?

How does suicide affect the people it leaves behind? They have feelings of sorrow and loss, guilt that they didn't know or couldn't help, etc.

How does suicide affect our society? It makes life seem meaningless; it encourages others to do the same thing, etc.

How has suicide affected someone you know?

Why do you think people turn to suicide? They feel hopeless; they are trying to get attention; they are on drugs, trying to get revenge, etc.

What kinds of situations make people feel desperate enough to kill themselves? It could be something as serious as hearing you have a terminal disease to something as simple as not being invited to a party—anything that sends someone over the edge of his or her tolerance.

When have you felt desperate, as if there's no way out?

How do you think God feels about suicide?

What do you think can keep a person from committing suicide? Having someone to talk to, someone who understands their pain or suffering.

Transition to the next step by explaining: **We all face desperate times when we may feel like there's no way out but suicide. But suicide is never the only option, and it never solves a problem. As we'll see today, we can go to Jesus for help when we're desperate.**

Option 3 Fun and Games

You'll need A stopwatch (or a watch with a seconds indicator).

Greet students and divide them into two teams. Instruct students on one team to join hands and form a circle around the other team. Explain that you are going to use the stopwatch to time how long it takes the team inside the circle to break through (no hitting, kicking or knocking anyone over).

Begin the game and keep track of the time it takes for the team on the inside to get outside the circle; then have teams switch places. After the second team has broken through, announce the winning team; then discuss:

How did it feel to be the inside team?

What was it like to be the outside team?

How was this game similar to desperate times we face in life? It often feels like we are struggling to get out of a difficult time.

In real life, what kinds of situations make us feel desperate, as if there's no way out? Failure, illness, parents' divorce, rejection, loss of something or someone important to us, depression, etc.

Transition by explaining: **We all experience desperate times, and in those times, suicide may seem like the only real way out. But it's never the right answer. As we'll see today, we can go to Jesus instead.**

This step reassures students that there's always hope in Jesus.

You'll need Several Bibles, paper and pens or pencils.

Explain: **In Matthew 26, we find out that Judas, one of the 12 original disciples, betrayed Jesus and turned Him over to people sent by the Jewish leaders to arrest Him.** Ask for nine volunteers to play the following parts: Judas, Jesus, two priests, a disciple of Jesus, the field, two coins and the temple. Explain that as you read Matthew 27:1-10, the volunteers should act out exactly what is happening. Warn them that if they don't do a convincing job, the crowd will yell out "Do it again!" and they'll have to do it all over.

> **Note:** If you don't have enough volunteers to give each one a separate role, double or triple up on some of the roles. That might make for an interesting performance!

When students have finished the drama, discuss:
Why do you think Judas committed suicide?
How do you think he was feeling?
What other options did he have? He needed to turn to God for forgiveness.
Read Luke 23:39-43 and discuss:
How did the criminal find hope in his desperate situation? He realized he was a sinner and asked Jesus to remember him.
How did his life change when he turned to Jesus? He was promised eternal life.
How is this different than Judas? Judas died in sin; he didn't acknowledge that Jesus was God.
What kind of hope does Jesus offer people in desperate situations? He will be there for them, helping them through the tough times. He suffered betrayal, injustice, an illegal trial, numerous beatings and a terrible, cruel death for *our* sins—that's how much He loves us and how much He understands our pain.

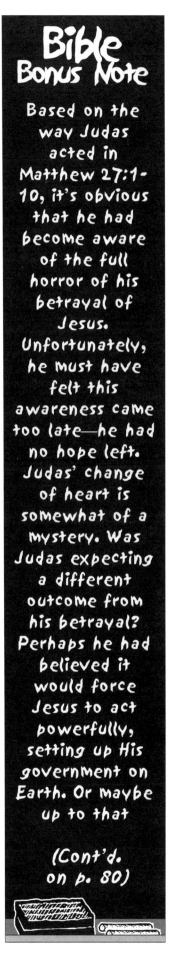

Bible Bonus Note

Based on the way Judas acted in Matthew 27:1-10, it's obvious that he had become aware of the full horror of his betrayal of Jesus. Unfortunately, he must have felt this awareness came too late—he had no hope left. Judas' change of heart is somewhat of a mystery. Was Judas expecting a different outcome from his betrayal? Perhaps he had believed it would force Jesus to act powerfully, setting up His government on Earth. Or maybe up to that

(Cont'd. on p. 80)

Bible Bonus Note

(Cont'd. from p. 79)

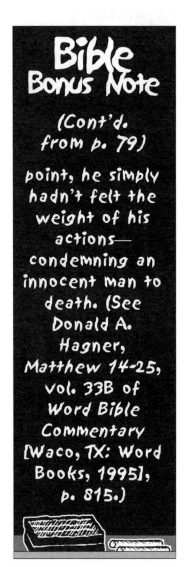

point, he simply hadn't felt the weight of his actions—condemning an innocent man to death. (See Donald A. Hagner, *Matthew 14-25*, vol. 33B of *Word Bible Commentary* [Waco, TX: Word Books, 1995], p. 815.)

Option 2
Chat Room

You'll need Several Bibles, paper and pens or pencils.

Distribute Bibles and explain: **In Matthew 26, we find out that Judas, one of the 12 original disciples, betrayed Jesus and turned Him over to people sent by the Jewish leaders to arrest Him.** Ask three volunteers to read Matthew 27:1-10 in turn, with one volunteer playing the narrator, another reading what Judas says and the third reading what the priests say. After the reading, discuss:

How do you think Judas was feeling?

Why did he choose suicide? He probably couldn't live with the guilt of what he had done.

What was the result of his choice? He died without the forgiveness of Jesus.

What might have happened if he had turned to Jesus instead? Because he would have known that he was forgiven, he might have become the greatest witness for the message of the gospel—much like Paul who had been responsible for the deaths of Christians.

What kind of hope could Jesus have offered Judas? Forgiveness for his sins, eternal life.

Read Luke 23:39-43 and discuss:

How did the criminal find hope in his desperate situation? He realized he was a sinner and asked Jesus to remember him.

How did his life change when he turned to Jesus? He was promised eternal life.

How is this different than Judas? Judas died in sin; he didn't acknowledge that Jesus was God.

What kind of hope does Jesus offer people in desperate situations? He will be there for them, helping them through the tough times. He suffered betrayal, injustice, an illegal trial, numerous beatings and a terrible, cruel death for *our* sins—that's how much He loves us and how much He understands our pain.

What might you say to someone considering suicide?

Option 3

Pulse Points

You'll need A white board, a dry-erase marker, a window pane, mud (otherwise known as dirt and water), a clean soft cloth, window cleaner and a telephone.

Ahead of time, dirty the window pane with the mud enough so that it will be hard to see through, but not so dirty that you can't clean it in 30 to 60 seconds.

The Big Idea
There's always hope in Jesus.

The Big Question
What kind of hope does Jesus offer?

1. Jesus offers a master plan.

Read Matthew 27:1-10 and explain: **Judas didn't know that God was in control of the situations around him and was working out His master plan for the world.**

Ask students: **What were Judas's other options? What could he have done instead of choosing to commit suicide?** List responses on the white board.

Continue: **If Judas had turned to Jesus, he would have experienced Jesus' purpose for coming to Earth—redemption and forgiveness. Eventually, he would have seen the bigger picture and the hope Jesus offered. God has a master plan for the world. He can change our circumstances in a heartbeat, and He can cause even the most tragic of situations to bring good in our lives.**

2. Jesus offers a fresh start.

Explain: **If Judas had turned to Jesus, he would have experienced forgiveness, and God would have made him a new person, giving him the strength he needed to begin to change.**

Ask a volunteer to read Luke 23:39-43. As the passage is read, use a clean soft cloth and some window cleaner to clean the windowpane.

Point out how clean and clear the windowpane is now and explain: **Jesus gives us a fresh start when we turn to Him. Our past sins are wiped away. He makes us new people. When we truly experience God's forgiveness and change in our lives, we can see clearly that suicide isn't the answer.**

3. Jesus offers His presence.

Explain: **When we turn to Jesus, He'll comfort us and give us wisdom.**

Hold up the telephone and conclude: **Having a relationship with Jesus is like having a good friend on the phone all the time. Jesus is always there for us, anywhere we go and no matter what our circumstances. And Jesus sometimes provides His presence through other people. He brings other people into our lives to offer help and hope, and it's important to turn to them when we need help.**

STEP 3 — MOVING ON

This step reveals Jesus' hope in our individual lives.

Option 1 — Chat Room

You'll need Paper and pens or pencils.

Divide students into pairs; then distribute paper and pens or pencils and instruct the pairs to look around and find an object that represents hope in Jesus. They can look in the room, in the building or even outside if you have enough adult supervision. When they find an object, they can write down its description and return to the group. (A few examples: a chair that represents how when we're tired, Jesus offers us rest, or a pencil sharpener that represents how when we get dull, Jesus keeps us sharp.)

Allow a few minutes for students to look and write; then bring the group back together and discuss:

How does your object symbolize hope in Jesus?

What kind of hope does Jesus offer? Ever-present hope, hope of eternal life with Him, etc.

When have you or someone else experienced hope in Jesus?

How does hope affect people's lives? It keeps them going when times are tough.

How does hopelessness affect people's lives? It makes them want to quit.

How can Jesus provide hope for people considering suicide? He can give them a reason to live—for Him and His kingdom. He can strengthen them in bad times.

How do we find hope in Jesus? By praying, reading the Bible, being around other hope-filled Christians, etc.

NOTES

You'll need Nothing but this story.

Share the following make-believe journal entry:

> **Dear Diary,**
>
> I just don't think life is worth living anymore. It finally happened—Chris broke up with me. I knew it was going to end soon, but I just didn't know how to stop it from happening.
>
> Now I have nobody. Nobody really understands me or knows how I feel. I don't even know how I feel. I'm just sort of numb or something.
>
> I wish I had just one friend who really knew me and liked me and who I could talk to. Nobody ever listens to what I have to say. My parents are too busy for me, and they have no clue what I'm going through.
>
> Sometimes at school, when I walk down the hall, I just feel like I'm invisible or something. No one seems to notice I'm there. The teachers only talk to me when I screw up on something.
>
> What's wrong with me? Why does everyone else seem to be happier than I am? I don't think I can go on living this way. Maybe I should just end it all—stop the pain, take myself out of everyone's way.

Encourage students to think about how this person could find hope in Jesus and discuss:

What are some options for this person, besides committing suicide? Talking to an adult who can help (such as a school counselor), calling a suicide hotline, talking to a pastor or youth leader or telling his or her parents how he or she feels. The point is to talk to *someone* about his or her feelings.

What would you say to help this person? I'm here to listen to you and I know someone who is always near you—Jesus. He loves you so much He gave His life for you.

How could Jesus bring hope into this person's life? He is always nearby, waiting to listen to your problems and help you when things are tough. He knows everything that has happened to you and what you are thinking.

Option 3  Tough Questions

You'll need Just these questions.

1. **What can we say to people who talk about committing suicide?** We can listen and share with them the hope we've experienced and refer them to people who can help them. It's important to take people seriously and to involve an adult who can give them counseling, instead of keeping it a secret.

Youth Leader Tip

It's possible that this lesson will prompt students to disclose to you that they're suicidal or that people they know are contemplating suicide. So what should you do if someone is suicidal?

According to the American Association of Suicidology, the most important thing is to show a willingness to talk to young people about their feelings. Affirm that it's OK for teenagers to talk with you about such things and that you accept them. And don't ever promise to keep secret what students share with you. You may need to break confidentiality to save a person's life.

Ask for some specific information: Has the person considered a method of suicide? Made any specific plans? Taken steps toward carrying out the plans?

Avoid such comments as "You just

(Cont'd. on p.83)

2. **How can we find Jesus' hope in this depressing world?** He provides hope all around us—often in places and ways we tend to take for granted because they're always there. We should actively look for and keep a record of places where we find hope, such as keeping a journal, videotaping or talking with others about the hope we experience.

3. **Does Jesus really provide hope for everyone? Aren't some people beyond it?** No one is beyond hope. Jesus is much bigger than our circumstances, and He can bring hope to any situation in any person's life.

4. **Why doesn't God stop people from committing suicide?** Sometimes He does, and sometimes He doesn't. He's allowed us all to have choices in life, and if we choose death, He doesn't force life on us.

5. **Why does God care if people commit suicide?** God cares about everyone—the people who kill themselves and the people they leave behind. He knows how much suicide hurts. He also knows that when people commit suicide, they've given up on Him. He wants us always to turn to Him for hope and meaning in life.

6. **Does God forgive people who commit suicide and let them into heaven?** On the basis of the sixth commandment—"You shall not murder" (Exodus 20:13)—some Christians have taught that a person committing suicide automatically goes straight to hell. However, this teaching conflicts with the center of the gospel: our eternal destiny has nothing to do with either our good works (i.e., avoiding suicide) or bad works (i.e., committing suicide) but rather on God's grace through our faith in Christ (see Ephesians 2:8,9).

7. **What should I do if I think someone I know is seriously thinking about killing themselves? Should I tell someone?** Although it might feel like you're betraying him or her if you tell someone, the ultimate betrayal is to let someone hurt him- or herself. If you think someone is serious about committing suicide, tell your parent(s) or a trusted Christian adult and let them help you figure out what to do.

Youth Leader Tip

(Cont'd. from p.82)

don't appreciate how lucky you are" or "Think about how much better off you are than most people." Such comments only reinforce feelings of hopelessness and guilt.

Be sure to refer the suicidal student to a counselor, suicide prevention center or crisis intervention center. If a student refuses to reach out for help, talk with an expert yourself to get further advice. Also be ready to talk to the student's parents if his or her life is truly in danger. If someone seems to be in immediate danger, stay with the person until help arrives.

NOTES

STEP 4
MOVING OUT

This step gives students some tangible ways to celebrate life in Jesus.

Option 1 — Light the Fire

You'll need Paper and pens or pencils.

Explain that one of the things that can help when we are feeling depressed, or even suicidal, is to remember the things that God has done for us and the things we have to be grateful for. Distribute paper and pens or pencils and have students list things they are grateful for, coming up with as many items as there are years in their age (i.e., a 13-year-old would list 13 items).

If you have time, divide students into groups of four and have them share three things from their lists within their small groups. Close in prayer, thanking God for all He has done—that He is the Rock that we need in times of turmoil as well as times of ease!

Option 2 — Fired Up

You'll need Cake or another treat, drinks, party decorations, worship songs, accompaniment (optional), a large piece of paper or fabric and colored felt-tip pens.

Explain that students are going to have a spontaneous celebration of life in Jesus. Serve the treat and drinks and ask students help you decorate the room. When the room is decorated, spend time singing worship songs. While students are celebrating, place a large piece of paper or fabric where everyone can reach it and make the felt-tip pens available. Instruct students to use the pens and paper to create a mural of things that make life in Jesus worth living.

When the mural and the celebration are complete, discuss: **How can we celebrate life in Jesus *every* day?**

Gather around the mural and hold hands. Close in prayer, asking God to help you and your students cele-brate your lives in Jesus daily. Hang the mural in your meeting room as a reminder of hope in Jesus.

Option 3 — Spread the Fire

You'll need Helium-filled balloons, uninflated balloons and permanent fine-point, felt-tip pens **Note**: Some pens will eat through balloons, causing them to pop. Be sure to test one before you do this activity with your students!

Give each student one balloon filled with helium and invite them to use the felt-tip pens to write on their balloons descriptions or pictures of things that bring us hope and make life in Jesus worth living.

Allow a few minutes for writing; then lead a prayer thanking God for hope in Jesus. Invite students to take turns praying aloud while releasing their balloons to float to the ceiling.

After prayer, ask students to come up with ways to bring hope in Jesus to others who are discouraged or depressed. Some ideas might include: getting peer counselor training, listening to someone, smiling for no reason, reaching out to meet people, taking a stand, inviting someone to church, telling others about Christ, etc.

Allow several minutes for sharing; then give each student an uninflated balloon that they can blow up and use to write on, describing one way to bring hope in Jesus to others. Students should be willing to commit to bringing hope to others in the ways they write on their balloons.

Encourage students to take their balloons home and to begin fulfilling their commitments before their balloons deflate.

NOTES

Startling Statistics*

In 1997 . . .

There were 30,535 suicides in the United States. That means
> 84 suicides per day; or
> one suicide every 17 minutes.

Every suicide intimately affects at least 6 other people. That means
> over 500 new people every day grieved a loss due to suicide; or
> over 183,000 friends and family members in one year.

There were 4,186 people between the ages of 15 and 24 who committed suicide. That means
> over 11 suicides per day; or
> one suicide every 2 hours and 6 minutes which left 25,116 friends and family members to grieve in one year.

For every young person who committed suicide, 100 to 200 attempted it. That means
> between 418,600 and 837,200 young people attempted suicide *in one year.*

Suicide was the third leading cause of death among people ages 15 to 24. Compare this to
> the national ranking of suicide--eighth; and
> the national ranking of homicide--13th.

* Statistical data gathered from information found at American Association of Suicidology's Internet website at www.suicidology.org.

Devotions in Motion

WEEK SIX: SUICIDE

DAY 1

FAST FACTS

Take comfort when you turn to 2 Corinthians 12:9,10.

God Says

Jackie doesn't think much of herself. She's not athletic and doesn't get very good grades. Her older brothers and sisters have always been very successful, so she feels like she is not good enough. She thinks that if she were gone, nobody would miss her. She has contemplated suicide many times.

What Jackie forgets is that she is an incredible artist and a very good friend to people. I guess Jackie finds it easier to focus on the things she is not good at rather than the things she is good at.

I Do

God made us all unique. The way God thinks is so different from the way the world thinks. The world says we need to be good at everything. God says you need to be weak. He wants to use those weak areas, not to make you upset and down on yourself, but to teach you to rely on him.

What are the areas in your life that are weak spots?

How might God use you in your weak areas?

Tell God you want to be used in your weakness today.

FOLD HERE -

DAY 4

QUICK QUESTIONS

Have you ever read Acts 16:23-28? Well, turn there and read an amazing story.

God Says

Larissa overheard her parents talking. It seemed that her brother Jess was in big trouble. Her parents were discussing what to do with him. So Larissa went and told her brother what she had heard he had been having trouble at school but hadn't told his parents anything about it. He became very scared and thought about suicide as a way to get out of trouble with his parents.

Then Jess heard his dad's footsteps coming toward his room, and he knew he was about to be busted. But to Jess's surprise, his dad walked into his room, hugged him and asked about his day. Jess asked his dad if he was in trouble and his dad said No, what makes you think that?

Jess told him that Larissa had overheard them talking, but his dad explained that he had been talking about someone from work, not Jess.

I Do

Sometimes when we don't fully understand the truth of a situation, we can get mixed-up about it. Our emotions can run wild and we can find ourselves thinking some pretty bad thoughts—maybe even things like I want to kill myself.

What can you do to make sure you do not jump to conclusions?

How can God help you before you do something you'll regret?

QUICK QUESTIONS

What are you doing tomorrow? Read Matthew 6:34.

God Says

Charlie has had a horrible day. He just found out his parents are getting divorced and that he is flunking math. He wonders when—if ever—all of his problems will end. He is thinking about killing himself. What would you tell him?

I Do.

All of us are going to have hard times in life. Just because we are Christians does not mean that we never have hard times or bad days again. Sometimes we feel like the hard times or bad days will never get better, but that's not the truth.

What does the verse say about that?

What can you tell people who have no hope in tomorrow and think suicide is a good option?

FOLD HERE

FAST FACTS

Psalm 103:1,2 will change you, so find it fast!

God Says

Greg is very sick. He has been in the hospital for weeks and is frustrated. The doctors do not know what is wrong with him. Greg lies alone for most of the day and thinks. In the beginning he had thoughts of the time when he would get out of the hospital. Now he just thinks about how hard his life is. He has lost hope and would rather just die. Greg does not know who Jesus is, but someone brought him a Bible as a gift. The more he reads the Bible, the less he wants to die.

I Do.

Have you ever thought a situation was hopeless? What was so hopeless about it?

As Christians we are never without hope. We serve a God who heals and redeems us. Are you thankful for that? Spend the next 83 seconds thanking God for the hope He's given you—not just for your life now but also for the eternal life you have if you've asked Jesus to be your Savior.

How to Leave a Mark on Your School

Let's say you spend about 7 hours a day in school, 5 days a week. That's 35 hours per week. Then say you're in school approximately 40 weeks a year. Do the math and you'll find you're in school about 1,400 hours each school year! That's a lot of time spent in one place.

Now, don't get discouraged. Yes, that means a lot of teachers, books and tests—but it also means you have a tremendous opportunity to do something great for God. This thought may be new to you. You're probably used to thinking that school is about what you can get—soaking up everything you can learn before you get to the real world outside of school—not about what you can give. But school *is* a place you can give. You can leave a mark that will change lives (yours included!) and glorify God. Why? Jesus called His followers both salt and light (see Matthew 5:13-16). He meant that they were to be the seasoning among the scrambled eggs of people, the ones that stood out and made the rest taste better. And they were to be the light shining in the darkness of a very dark world.

In the last few years, schools have become pretty scary places. Your friends, your classmates, and even your teachers desperately need you to be salt and light. They need you to show them the way to Jesus.

Step One:
Develop Your Own Relationship with God

Light can't shine if it's under a barrel of sin, so in order to shine your light at school, first you need to have a growing relationship with Jesus. Don't try to be perfect; just love God with all you've got and all you are.

Step Two: Pray

Pray for your school, the administrators, the content taught in your classes, the faculty, your friends, classmates and other students. Find creative ways to pray. For instance, you could pray for one of the above each day of the week. You could pray using the days of the week—for example, pray for teachers and tests on Tuesday. (You'll have to be creative for those prayers that don't start with S, M, T, W or F!) Involve others in prayer and gather some friends to pray before school or during lunch. When people notice what you're doing, they may ask why you pray, and you'll have a great opportunity to share about Jesus. They may even ask to join you!

Step Three:
Live So That People See Jesus in You

After Jesus' resurrection, Peter and John were arrested for preaching about Him. The rulers were amazed that uneducated fishermen were able to defend themselves with such courage. Acts 4:13 says, "They took note that these men had been with Jesus." Jesus so affected Peter and John that others saw Jesus' power shining through them. You can have the same effect on others around you.

Step Four:

Treat People with Love

"Dear friends, since God so loved us, we also ought to love one another" (1 John 4:11). Jesus touched lost, lonely, hurting people. Jesus not only said that He loved the unlovable, but He *did* something about it. Try to imagine you're wearing "Jesus glasses" that allow you to see people the way Jesus does. Look for the outcasts. Look for people's needs and ask God how He wants you to love them. Making eye contact and offering a smile might be a good start. Or maybe you can help someone who's struggling in a class.

These steps may not sound revolutionary, but you don't have to start a campus club or stage a march (though you could!) to make an impact at school. Jesus started a revolution by loving and leading a small group of ordinary people. Following Jesus revolutionizes people's lives—if you point people to Him, He will make a difference at your school.

PIPING HOT RESOURCES FOR YOUTH WORKERS

Illustrations, Stories and Quotes to Hang Your Message On
Jim Burns & Greg McKinnon
Manual / 237p • ISBN 08307.18834 • $16.99

Worship Experiences
Jim Burns & Robin Dugall
Manual / 144p • ISBN 08307.24044 • $16.99

Missions and Service Projects
Jim Burns, General Editor
Manual / 121p • ISBN 08307.18796 • $16.99

Incredible Retreats
Jim Burns & Mike DeVries
Manual / 144p • ISBN 08307.24036 • $16.99

Games, Crowdbreakers and Community Builders
Jim Burns, Mark Simone & Joel Lusz
Manual / 219p • ISBN 08307.18818 • $16.99

Skits & Dramas
Jim Burns, General Editor
Manual / 172p • ISBN 08307.18826 • $16.99

Bible Study Outlines and Messages
Jim Burns & Mike DeVries
Manual / 219p • ISBN 08307. 18850 • $16.99

Case Studies, Talk Sheets and Discussion Starters
Jim Burns & Mark Simone
Manual / 125p • ISBN 08307.18842 • $16.99

Nobody Talks Your Teens' Language Like Jim Burns

YouthBuilders Group Bible Studies are a high-involvement, discussion-oriented, Bible-centered, comprehensive program for seeing teens through their high-school years and beyond. From respected youth worker Jim Burns. Reproducible!

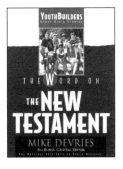

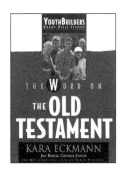

The Word on the Old Testament
Manual / 135p
ISBN 08307.17269 • $16.99

The Word on the New Testament
Manual / 170p
ISBN 08307.17250 • $16.99

The Word on Spiritual Warfare
ISBN 08307.17242 • $16.99

The Word on the Basics of Christianity
Manual / 245p
ISBN 08307.16440 • $16.99

The Word on the Sermon on the Mount
Manual / 148p
ISBN 08307.17234 • $16.99

The Word on Sex, Drugs & Rock 'N' Roll
Manual / 186p
ISBN 08307.16424 • $16.99

The Word on Family
ISBN 08307.17277 • $16.99

The Word on Helping Friends in Crisis
Manual / 223p
ISBN 08307.16467 • $16.99

The Word on Finding and Using Your Spiritual Gifts
Manual / 203p
ISBN 08307.17897 • $16.99

The Word on Prayer and the Devotional Life
Manual / 213p
ISBN 08307.16432 • $16.99

The Word on Being a Leader, Serving Others & Sharing Your Faith
Manual / 195p
ISBN 08307.16459 • $16.99

The Word on the Life of Jesus
Manual / 195p
ISBN 08307.16475 • $16.99

Available at your local Christian bookstore.

Gospel Light

041446